Anonymous

**The Path of the Pilgrim Church**

From its Origin in England to its Establishment in New England

Anonymous

**The Path of the Pilgrim Church**
*From its Origin in England to its Establishment in New England*

ISBN/EAN: 9783337293352

Printed in Europe, USA, Canada, Australia, Japan

Cover: Foto ©Lupo / pixelio.de

More available books at **www.hansebooks.com**

Pilgrim Church.

# THE PATH

OF

# THE PILGRIM CHURCH,

FROM ITS ORIGIN IN ENGLAND TO ITS ESTABLISH-
MENT IN NEW ENGLAND.

AN HISTORICAL SKETCH.

WRITTEN FOR THE MASSACHUSETTS SABBATH SCHOOL SOCIETY, AND
APPROVED BY THE COMMITTEE OF PUBLICATION.

BOSTON:
MASSACHUSETTS SABBATH SCHOOL SOCIETY,
DEPOSITORY, NO. 13 CORNHILL.

Entered, according to Act of Congress, in the year 1862,

BY THE MASSACHUSETTS SABBATH SCHOOL SOCIETY,

In the Clerk's Office of the District Court of Massachusetts.

Electrotyped and Printed by Wright & Potter, No. 4 Spring Lane.

# PREFACE.

It has seemed to the writer desirable that young persons should have a more distinct and *coherent* knowledge than is common, of the causes, influences, circumstances, trials, and providences connected with the emigration of our forefathers to their home in New England. It has accordingly been his aim to enable his readers to look in upon those transactions and see them as they were. It would have been easy to expand the narrative; but he has aimed at brevity. Some of the topics would have required a fuller statement, had the volume been written for a different class of readers. Some portions of the book may even now seem too circumstantial—for example, the account given of the principles of the Puritans. But the statement was thought to be as brief as it could consistently be made.

# PREFACE.

The writer is well aware that he could have made, in some respects, a more spirited narrative, by casting much of his material into other forms of statement. But he thought it better on the whole to let the actors, in great measure, tell their own tale, and to secure perfect truthfulness rather than graphic effect. The narrative is a history, and not a fancy sketch. Even the wanting links of the story have not been supplied, except in cases perfectly obvious. The facts have been gathered with care from various sources, such as Bradford's History of Plymouth Plantation, Young's Chronicles, Neal's History of the Puritans, Hunter's Founders of New Plymouth, Bartlett's Plymouth and the Pilgrims, Motley's Dutch Republic, and various other volumes.

# CONTENTS.

| CHAPTER. | PAGE. |
|---|---|
| I.—SCROOBY MANOR, | 7 |
| II.—HAMPTON COURT, | 27 |
| III.—STAR CHAMBER AND HIGH COMMISSION, | 52 |
| IV.—BOSTON AND HULL, | 66 |
| V.—HOLLAND, | 78 |
| VI.—LEYDEN, | 107 |
| VII.—LONDON, | 131 |
| VIII.—DELFT HAVEN, | 148 |
| IX.—THE OCEAN, | 163 |
| X.—THE LAND, | 183 |
| XI.—HOME, | 201 |
| XII.—FAST AND THANKSGIVING, | 225 |
| XIII.—REST AT LAST, | 241 |

# PATH OF THE PILGRIM CHURCH.

## CHAPTER I.

### SCROOBY MANOR.

Not more than a mile from the boundary line between the counties of York and Nottingham, in England, and six miles west of Lincolnshire, lies the little village of Scrooby. Though situated on a branch of the Northern Railway, it is quite too small a village to be found upon an ordinary map. It lies in the midst of a level and fertile district. The fields around, neatly divided by green hedges, are laden in summer with heavy crops of grain, or dotted here and there with grazing cattle. Through the plain slowly and glassily winds the little stream well termed the Idle, lingering in many a curve on its way to join the Trent. To the north a little way beyond the Idle lies the village of Austerfield, hidden among the trees from the sight of the railway traveler; while the site of Scrooby, close upon its southern bank, is marked at once to the eye by the village church pointing with its graceful spire to the sky.

One spot about the village of Scrooby— and one alone—possesses special interest. Even that has very little for the eye to see. Passing the modest cottages and along the rich grassy plain that skirts the river, through a wicket gate you enter a large enclosure covered with the finest turf, bounded on one side by the river and on another by the railroad. A trench or moat, now dry, but which within the memory of living men was filled with water, divides the enclosure from the gardens of the village; and near the centre of the area stands a noble group of sycamores. Nothing remains to tell of the wealth and luxury that once reveled on this spot, except a few fragments of richly carved wood-work which, a few years since, and perhaps now, might be seen sustaining the roof of a neighboring cow-house.

That dry moat, and that carved wood work carry us back to a time when for several generations the archbishops of York used to ride forth from this spot with their splendid retinues to the chase, and return at night to the festive board. For that forsaken spot was once occupied by Scrooby Manor House, the favorite hunting-seat of the Primates of England. The group of sycamores, no doubt, stands near the site of the principal building. An odd-looking pile it must have been—an "inner court-building" encompassed by a spacious outer court four times as large, all built of timber, except the front of the house—the latter being of brick, with a flight of stone steps leading to the door. The whole was surrounded by a moat.

Royalty once at least had mounted that stone stairway. In 1541 Henry the Eighth, on his northward journey, had passed a night at Scrooby Manor. But his presence can hardly have added to the pleasure of the palace; for it was towards the close of his life, a few months before the lustful tyrant, who had divorced two wives and beheaded one, executed yet another. They must have breathed more freely in the manor as he passed on his way.

But the time came when the old manor house was to be thronged with a very different company. The last archbishop that resided here was the learned but hasty and passionate Sandys, a vigorous hater of the Puritans. When the old man died in 1588, the estate was bequeathed to his son, Sir Samuel Sandys, thenceforth to be more and more neglected, till the park became a farm and the house fell to decay. But before decay had begun its work, and while the archbishop's son still owned it, though he did not occupy, the ancient halls began to echo with unwonted sounds. On each Sabbath morning, as early at least as the year 1606, a watchful observer might have seen a considerable number of men and women, quietly and even stealthily gathering from the villages around, and entering the old manor house. A grave but cheerful man, some forty years of age, with a deliberate utterance and the air of one who had mingled with men, welcomed his brethren in the Lord. It was WILLIAM BREWSTER—a man whom God had specially guided, and trained, and brought to this spot for the work in which he was now engaged, of gathering up the Puritan spirit of the neighboring country—of making *Scrooby Manor the cradle of the Pilgrim Church*, and thenceforth of daring and enduring foremost in all the checkered fortunes of the church, and aiding its business affairs with his practical wisdom and firmness, till the little church was landed and firmly planted in its western home.

William Brewster—"Elder Brewster," as he afterwards became—seems to have been all along the central person of the enterprise, the man to whose influence, judgment and firmness the church was most indebted in all its earlier outward history. He was of what is called a good family—had been well educated, and even spent a little time at Cambridge University, where he became a religious man. Thence he had entered the service of Sir William Davison, Secretary of State to Queen Elizabeth—a man of rare qualities and true piety. He had been Davison's confidential servant and friend, had accompanied him on his embassy to the Netherlands—had slept with the Keys of Flushing under his pillow—had ridden through England wearing his master's gold chain of honor, on their return—and when the false queen had executed her own cousin, Mary of Scotland, and thrown the blame upon her Secretary, Brewster still followed him in his fall till his good offices could be of no further use. The next we hear of him he has retired to the country and rented the old manor at Scrooby. For thirteen years, at least, he held the office of postmaster, or post, as the term then was, at Scrooby. It was a busy office. His work was not alone to receive and deliver letters and transmit them over the great northern mail route, but to send them by special despatches into the region round, not provided then, as now, with cross-routes, to keep relays of horses for travelers *by post*, and to furnish such travelers the rest and refreshment they might require. It was a sort of compound of the business of postmaster, expressman and innkeeper. His business will explain his occupancy of so large a mansion. But while his head and hands are full of work, his heart is full of Christian zeal. Besides his own godly life and example, he is active in "procuring good preachers to all places thereabouts, and drawing on of others to assist and help to forward in such a work; he himself being commonly deepest in the charge, and sometimes above his ability."

But the time has arrived when he and his friends can no longer worship in the parish churches. Their conscientious piety is "scoffed and scorned," the godly ministers that fed the flame of their faith are driven out of the churches and forbidden to preach, and the people themselves are hunted and harrassed by the civil authorities, as will presently appear, till they will soon be fairly driven to make a firm and final stand. They met informally to pray and praise, till at length, about the time when we have introduced Brewster to the reader—not earlier than 1602, and probably as late as 1606—they have joined themselves into a church of Christ, and agree to walk in all his ways "whatsoever it should cost them." It was a costly experiment to them. And Brewster is the central spirit in the movement, and is to be the one fertile and resolute character around whom the whole enterprise hinges.

So here they are, strangely enough, in the old episcopal mansion. And while in the neighboring church a surpliced priest is chanting prayers to the swell of the organ, or reciting a sermon that he never composed, or reading the daily lessons from the apocrypha, or, clad in a cope, is administering the wafer-bread to kneeling men profane in speech and godless in life, and while the people are bowing at every mention of the name of Jesus, soon to retire from church and keep the remainder of the Lord's own day at the ale-house or the dancing-green— the little group at the manor house are praying without a book, and singing without an organ, and listening to the fervid words of one who speaks from his own deep religious experience to theirs, and then they will withdraw to their homes, to spend the rest of the sacred time with their families and train the little ones to count the day of the Lord honorable and a delight.

There are two preachers in that congregation to-day. One of them is "a grave and fatherly old man, having a great white beard." His name is Richard Clifton. Two or three miles away is the village church of Babworth and the pleasant parish where for many years he pungently preached the gospel and faithfully catechized the little ones, and led many souls to Christ. He has given up his pleasant home for his Master's sake—but he will die before this little flock find their new home beyond the Atlantic. His awakening ministry had penetrated into the neighboring villages before he left his Rectory, and one young man at least had habitually walked from Austerfield to Babworth to be enlightened in the gospel.

But the younger preacher of that Scrooby congregation is the man of mark. He is just thirty-one years old, and his name is destined to be memorable and venerable in the future church of God—it is JOHN ROBINSON. The little company do not know him yet as they soon will know him; for the company are mostly of Mr. Clifton's former congregation, and Robinson has just come among them. Of his personal appearance no record or hint remains. They soon found him to be "very courteous, affable and sociable in his conversation"—"a man learned and of solid judgment, and of a quick, sharp wit, of a tender conscience, and very sincere in all his ways—a hater of hypocrisy and dissimulation," and one who "would be very plain with his best friends." "He was an acute and expert disputant, very quick and ready;" a truth-loving man, "never satisfied till he had searched a cause to the bottom," and "ever desirous of any light." He soon became and always remained "much beloved" by his people, "and as loving was he unto them;" while he was also "much esteemed and reverenced of all that knew him." He is a graduate of Cambridge, has been rector of an Episcopal church, and abandoned it for conscience' sake. He is a man of more liberal and elevated views, perhaps, than any of his brethren, and soon to become in the spiritual affairs of the church what Brewster was in the temporal—"a man," say they in later times, "not easily to be paralleled."

One other person present demands especial attention, although but seventeen years of age. It is WILLIAM BRADFORD, the future historian of the little church and Governor of Plymouth Colony. Fourteen years ago his father died and left him to the guardianship of his uncles. He belongs to one of the most respectable families among the yeomanry of Austerfield. The little parish church still stands, in our day, seven or eight hundred years old, where in his childhood he attended service on the Sabbath. But at length the rumor of Clifton's awakening preaching reaches Austerfield and draws young Bradford thither. The way to Babworth, six or seven miles, lay through the village of Scrooby; and Brewster doubtless must often have been his companion on the latter portion of the road, and communed with him of heavenly things, as they went and came together. Amid the displeasure of friends and scoffs of the profane, he joins the little church, casts in his fortunes with it, and, young as he is, becomes one of its most efficient arms from this time forth. His early instructions must have been limited; but he has a thirst for knowledge, and will go on until he speaks the Dutch and the French languages, and has learned the Latin and the Greek; nor will he rest till he can read the Hebrew too, because he " will see with his own eyes the oracles of God in their native beauty." Resolute, prompt, self-denying, sagacious, modest and conciliatory—the time is coming when for six-and-thirty years, with but five years' rest, procured by his own earnest entreaty, he shall be Governor of the Colony at Plymouth.

The other faces are indistinct. Here very likely are Mr. Clifton's sons Zachary and Timothy, and in all probability Elder Brewster's children, at least the older ones, Patience, Fear, Love, and Wrestling. Here also, most likely, are Richard Jackson and Robert Rochester, though they are not to find their way to America. Here, perhaps, is Alice Carpenter, afterwards Mrs. Southworth, and her father. And could we look in upon them, no doubt we should see others who followed the fortunes of the little church to its haven of rest. But we have no certain knowledge who else at this time were here.

But why are they here at all? There are religious services to-day in the village church, scarcely a stone's throw away—the place where their fathers worshiped, the place where the villagers still assembled to listen to the liturgy and hear the hymns of praise chanted to the organ; yea, the very priest that reads those prayers they themselves are taxed to pay. Why then are they not there? Why does the old manor house echo their homelier strains of sacred song, and their louder words of petition and of exhortation? And why, too, if they preferred to worship thus, did they not continue quietly to assemble in this secluded spot, and not incur the trouble, the expense, and the trials of a journey to a distant land?

For those who live in a country and an age in which churches of every name are scattered peacefully around by each other's side, and every man, unmolested, attends on any or none of them all, according to his choice, it is hard to realize that those simple-hearted men who only met to worship God in their own chosen way, were offending against the highest authority of the realm, because they worshiped God in the old manor house rather than the village church, or that their preachers were incurring the punishment of felons because they thus dispensed the pure gospel of Christ without the prayer-book and the priestly robes and the village church. Yet so it was. And it required no little Christian hardihood, even for those who sympathized in their views, to take the decided stand. There was now but one other church like this in that portion of the kingdom—at Gainsborough, some ten miles distant.

Indeed it is not certain that there was a third like theirs now holding religious services in any portion of the kingdom. There had been a noble band that were accustomed to meet for prayer and reading of the Word of God in Southwark, a borough of London on the south side of the Thames, seeking privacy in the darkness of the night or the seclusion of some grove. They too had organized a church as early as 1592, at the house of Francis Johnson. But hardly had they done so, before the storm of persecution had burst upon them. Some fifty-nine of them lay at one time in various London prisons, besides ten of their number who had died in prison, sinking under the intentionally aggravated hardships and privations of their prison life. Henry Barrowe, John Greenwood and John Penry had been carried from those prisons to the gallows. Many of them had fled to Holland, till, between imprisonment and exile, the Southwark church had been suspended.

One link, at least, connected this persecuted band with the Scrooby church. The Rev. John Smyth, who had been a companion and fellow-sufferer of the Southwark brethren, was one of the ministers at Gainsborough; and from this latter flock the Scrooby church seems to have been an offshoot.

The tempest indeed had lulled after the murder of Greenwood, Barrow and Penry. No doubt there was hope of better times, when a change of monarchs should come and the sceptre should pass from the hands of stern Elizabeth. For it was during the year 1602—the last moody and broken-hearted year of the queen's life, not very far from the time when, though dying, she declared with characteristic energy that " no rascal's son but a king's," namely, "our cousin of Scotland" should succeed her,—that the Gainsborough church had been formed. The better times they looked for did not come. After a time—perhaps before the time at which this narrative commences—Smyth and many of the church at Gainsborough had left for Amsterdam.

The Scrooby church, in its secluded spot, remained the longest. Some favor may have been procured for them by the owner of the mansion—for another member of the family, Sir Edwin Sandys, ten years later, proved a valuable friend at court. But they were not unmolested. The malice of their adversaries first obliged them to change about their place of assembly, and "they kept their meetings every Sabbath in one place or another, exercising the worship of God among themselves," till they saw "they could no longer continue in that condition." Many of them "had their houses beset and watched night and day," and some "were taken and clapped up in prisons," until they too, "seeing there was no hope of their continuance there, by joint consent resolved to go into Holland."

But who was the man and what the influence that made their situation so intolerable? It was all summed up in one memorable sentence of the man who was "no rascal's son, but a king's," when he rose from his chair at Hampton Court and declared, "I will make them conform, or I will harry them out of the land, or else worse."

To the explanation afforded by that memorable scene we will look in the next chapter,—in which we must carry the reader back to a period three years previous.

# CHAPTER II.

### HAMPTON COURT.

On the north bank of the Thames, twelve miles nearly west of London, stands the palace of Hampton Court. It was once the favorite resort of the monarchs of England. It is now an odd architectural jumble, where the noble Tudor-Gothic of the original edifice, as built by Cardinal Wolsey, stands side by side with Grecian pillars and porticos, added by Sir Christopher Wren. It is now noted chiefly for its fine gardens and park, and for its gallery of a thousand pictures— many of them indeed of very little value, though containing a series of portraits of the successive Courts from Henry Eighth to George the Second, and above all, the seven celebrated cartoons of Raphael, which are among the chief wonders of ancient and modern art.

You could not have seen all these things there, of course, two hundred and fifty years ago. But if you had been there on Saturday, the 14th day of January, 1604, you would have beheld a very singular scene. In the drawing-room of the privy-chamber of this palace, there were gathered a showy group of men, the chief ecclesiastical and civil dignitaries of England. First and foremost were the three men who, eleven years before, had urged on the slaughter of Greenwood and Barrowe—namely, John Whitgift, Archbishop of Canterbury and Primate of all England, Richard Bancroft, the Bishop of London, his chief adviser and bitter successor, and Bilsin, Bishop of Winchester. With them were the bishops of Worcester, St. David's, Chichester, Carlisle, and Peterborough, one archdeacon and seven deans;

and around them stood the whole privy council of the king, and a numerous crowd of courtiers—spectators of the coming scene. A little forward of the canopy of state stood a vacant chair. As this brilliant group, all clad in their official costumes, had been summoned from the outer chamber to the drawing-room, they left behind them, in the ante-chamber, *sitting on a form* like a set of school-boys, four men, robed in fur gowns like the professors in foreign universities. All that day they were kept without. They bore the nickname, "Puritans."

When all was ready in the drawing-room, the king entered and seated himself, with his hat on, in the vacant chair—James the First of England, thirty-seven years of age, whom Mr. Dickens has described as "ugly, awkward and shuffling both in mind and person. His tongue was much too large for his mouth, his legs were much too weak for his body, and his dull, goggle-eyes stared and rolled like an idiot's. He was cunning, covetous, wasteful, idle, drunken, greedy, dirty, cowardly, and the most conceited man on earth. His figure—what is commonly called ricketty from his birth—presented the most ridiculous appearance that can be imagined, dressed in thick padded clothes, as a safeguard against being stabbed, (of which he lived in continual fear,) of a grass-green color from head to foot, with a hunting-horn dangling at his side instead of a sword, and his hat and feather sticking over one eye, or hanging on the top of his head as he happened to toss it on. He used to loll on the necks of his favorite courtiers, and slobber their faces, and kiss and pinch their cheeks; and the greatest favorite he ever had used to sign himself in letters to his royal master his majesty's 'dog and slave,' and used to address his majesty as 'his Sowship.' He was one of the most impertinent talkers ever heard, (in the broadest Scotch,) and boasted that he was unanswerable in argument." The picture is hardly overdrawn. The king was very disgusting in manners, and very conceited and despotic in character. He had considerable learning and no wisdom. He was here to display his conceit, his pedantry, his folly, and his despotism.

James had just ascended the throne of England nine months before. On his way to London, he was met by a petition called the " Millenary Petition," because signed by *near* a thousand ministers of the church of England, in which they humbly prayed for the " reformation of certain ceremonies and abuses of the church." James, in reply, had published a proclamation, appointing a conference, in which he would hear the parties desiring and those opposing the change. *He himself had nominated the disputants* on both sides. The time had now come; and here is the famous Conference of Hampton Court.

The king sits down in his chair. The church dignitaries in their canonicals stand before him. The courtiers and privy councillors look on. The four "Puritans" sit on their form in the ante-chamber. The king opens with a speech, in which he thanks God—and here he puts off his hat— that he is now come into the promised land; that he sits among grave and reverend men; that he is not a king as formerly [in Scotland] without state, nor in a place where beardless boys would brave him to his face. He assures them that he intends no essential changes in the church, though he is willing to remove any scandalous disorders; and if the complaints are frivolous, he " desires to cast a sop into Cerberus' mouth that he may never bark again." He then proceeds himself to make a few objections to certain things in the liturgy and practice of the established church. The bishops fall upon their knees and entreat the king not to consent to any alterations, lest it should be regarded as affixing a stigma on their past treatment of the Puritans. Three slight changes in the phraseology of the prayer-book are agreed upon. And so ends the first day's conference—which was merely a private arrangement between the king and one party as to the best mode of silencing the other.

Monday comes. The mock conference goes on. The four men in fur gowns are now called in—to be interrupted, sneered at, brow-beaten, threatened, and silenced. The ecclesiastics are there to break in upon them continually and vexatiously. The nobles and privy councillors are present to join occasionally in the "king's mirth and raillery" about the Puritans. The monarch himself is there to play the part of witness, advocate, and judge, and at times to add the authority of the sovereign. The four men are very able men, but they are abashed and intimidated as they stand in that presence, like culprits before a tribunal. Dr. Rainolds, professor at Oxford, is esteemed the most learned man in England; Dr. Sparke, another Oxford professor, and Mr. Chadderton, master of Emanuel College, Cambridge, are two very eminent scholars; and Mr. Knewstubbs, fellow of Cambridge University, a man of less prominence. They do not, however, fully represent the principles of the "thousand" ministers, nor are they in all respects agreed among themselves. But it makes little difference in the result.

These learned men did not succeed, even had they been fully prepared, in laying the whole case before the king. We will therefore gather up from various public statements made just about that time, within a year or two, the principal things they demanded, and lay them before the reader.

The main thing that covered the whole ground was this. "All that we crave of his majesty and the state is, that, with his and their permission, it may be lawful for us *to worship God according to his revealed will; and that we may not be* FORCED *to the observance of any human rites and ceremonies.*" Here is the whole thing in a nutshell—permission to worship God in their own way—according to the Scriptures, and without any human inventions. They do not ask to force any body else to their mode—they even say about this time that they are willing to pay their tithes or taxes for the support of the established churches. They only ask to be let alone.

Now, as we said, the "Puritans" did not all agree in every thing; nor did they all carry out the principle that they started with. But those that went farthest—to whom belong Robinson and Brewster and others, take the following ground.

They hold, then, that none but the Word of God can teach them what to believe and what ceremonies to use in worship; that it is very wrong for men to *compel* others to worship in any particular way; and also that it is wrong to use the ceremonies that men have invented, if they have been used in idolatry and superstition.

As a consequence of this freedom from compulsion, they hold one set of worshipers (or church) is equal in authority to any other church—and is not under its power, nor has any power over it. It must simply govern itself.

Every little church therefore must choose and have its own pastor and church officers. And there are no other church officers than those of particular churches—no bishops, archbishops, and the like.

Every pastor ought to be able to interpret the Word of God and to preach publicly; and all ignorant and mere reading priests ought to be rejected. He ought to be able himself to lead the congregation in prayer; and no forms or ceremonies, except those appointed in the Bible, ought to be laid upon him.

When a pastor is chosen, or an unworthy member is to be disciplined, it ought to be done with the free consent of the *whole church*.

When an unworthy member is finally excommunicated from the church, that is the end of the church's dealings with him, for " we exclude from ourselves all secular pomp or power, holding it a sin to punish men in their bodies, goods, liberties or lives, for any merely spiritual offence." \*

These principles in their full extent were held only by the smaller portion of the thousand ministers—the Independent or Congregational portion as they afterwards became, and to whom the Scrooby church

\* Neal I., 250.

belonged. Nor did *they* always consistently carry out their principles. The greater part, most likely, and *at that time* possibly Robinson himself, would have been satisfied with less radical changes, and remained in the Church of England.

The four Puritans at Hampton Court confined themselves to requests for certain improvements on the established church. They were not suffered to say all that they wanted to say. The things which they said and would have said, by way of objection to the church in which they were compelled to worship, were these:

They would have objected to the whole discipline of the Church of England, as unscriptural. All sorts of characters, the most wicked and abandoned, were admitted indiscriminately to the communion; and if a man were ever excommunicated, it was not done for any thing immoral, but because he would not comply with the ceremonies.

When excommunicated, it was done by a set of worldly men, not by the church or its spiritual officers; and the excommunication was only another name for fines, imprisonments, and confiscation of goods. No attempt was made to hallow the Sabbath, but trading and all sorts of amusements were freely allowed, and indeed soon after this by royal proclamation were openly encouraged.

They objected to the government of the church. They believed that all pastors were "bishops," and equal in authority. They claimed that to put the whole government of the church into the hands of a few men called archbishops, bishops, and so forth, and to give them power over their brethren and over the churches, was wholly contrary to the Bible. They held that the enormous incomes of these men who were not pastors, were wrong, while the poor pastors were many of them almost starved. They held that their worldly engagements and their pomp and parade were unscriptural—the very archbishop Whitgift then present having on one occasion entered Canterbury with a retinue of five hundred horsemen, one hundred of whom were his own servants. These officers were appointed, not by the churches, but by the king.

They objected to the way in which the churches were provided with ministers; that a certain man, perhaps a layman, would receive the income of a church, or of several churches, and hire some other person (a curate) to do his work; and these men so employed were, in a vast number of cases, too ignorant to prepare a sermon. The people had no voice in the selection of a pastor. They held that every minister should be qualified to preach; and moreover that he was the proper person to administer "confirmation," rather than the bishop, a stranger. They thought that the ministers should have permission to hold occasional meetings with each other for mutual improvement, called "prophesyings."

In regard to the church service, there were many things, more or less important, to which they took exception. It seemed wrong to be *compelled* always to use in public worship certain set forms of prayer, without permission in any case to express their petitions in their own words. Certain passages in the offices of baptism and burial, implying that the infant was regenerated in baptism, and that the deceased person had surely gone to heaven, they regarded as improper in doctrine. They held that the church "lessons," omitting, as they then did, nearly one-fourth of the Old Testament and substituting three-fifths of the Apocrypha, put dishonor on the inspired Word of God, and taught some grave errors. They regarded the observance of saints' days and church holidays as unauthorized and superstitious. The frequent repetition of the Lord's prayer and the constant responses did not please them, as savoring too much of vain repetitions; and especially they disproved of the "intoning" or singing of the prayers.

They had strong objections to certain required rites and ceremonies—some of them as being improper of themselves, others as having been connected with gross superstitions and tending to foster them. When a child was baptized it seemed to them utterly wrong that certain other parties than the parents should stand as godfathers and godmothers, and make those promises for the children which belonged only to the parents to make and to keep; also that a child should be entitled to the communion just as soon as it could repeat the Lord's prayer and the catechism, *without any other qualification.* The sign of the cross in baptism, which was no necessary part of the rite, and which had been so abused that many deemed the rite invalid without it, they disliked. Also the act of kneeling to receive the sacrament, as being a relic of the Romish superstition, which supposed the bread to be changed into the body of the Son of God and adored it accordingly—" a breaden God." They objected to being required to bow at the name of Jesus, as founded on a false interpretation of Scripture. They strongly disliked the surplice and other priestly vestments, because they had been consecrated to idolatrous and superstitious uses, and were the very badges and marks of the false religion which they themselves had renounced; the use of them gave a kind of countenance to popery, and was a great offence to weak minds. On similar grounds they were not well pleased with some other things that have now lost all unfavorable associations, as the ring in marriage, and organs and other musical instruments in church services.

In regard to these ceremonies, they objected above all to making them, as they were made, *absolutely compulsory;* and to ejecting a man from the ministry and forbidding him to preach at all, unless he subscribed to all the articles and ways of the church, and practiced all these ceremonies. This was the odious and tyrannical thing.

Such were the main things the Puritans asked. Some of them were of less importance and of temporary significance; others were of the deepest consequence. Some of them have since been weeded out of the English established Church, others modified —while some of the most serious difficulties still remain there.

The truth was, the Church of England was then but half reformed from the Romish Church. The English prayer-book was the Romish missal cleared of prayers to the

Virgin Mary, invocations of the saints, the more modern rites of the Romish Church, and some other excrescences; but a good many taints of its origin hung about it, and still hang about it to the present day. And at the time when James held this famous Conference, the condition of the Church was still unsettled. In fact when Henry Eighth broke off from the Church of Rome, the cause had been simply a question of power between him and the pope; who should govern in church matters in England? Henry just stepped into the pope's place, became head of the English Church, and had every thing in his own way. Elizabeth had stood in much the same position, and was in many respects quite as much a Catholic as a Protestant in her notions and feelings, to the day of her death. And now James was anxious to wield the same heavy rod of arbitrary power. Great hopes had been entertained of him by the Puritans, before he came to the throne. He had talked very differently while king of Scotland. He had praised the Scotch (Presbyterian) Church as the " sincerest kirk in the world," signed the " Confession of Faith," declared the service of the Church of England to be " an evil-said mass in English," and once interposed with Elizabeth in behalf of the Puritans in England. But in the words of Mr. Hallam, "James was all his life rather a bold liar than a good dissembler."

So he turns at Hampton Court to the lords and bishops with the words, " I will tell you I have lived among this sort of men ever since I was ten years old, but I may say of myself, as Christ said of himself, ' Though I have lived among them, yet, since I had ability to judge, I never was of them.' " Accordingly, the conference was all a sham.

James calls on the four doctors for their objections. Dr. Rainolds begins his reply.

Before he gets far, Bishop Bancroft, "in a heat," on his knees begs the king "to stop the doctor's mouth, because schismatics are not to be heard against their bishops." Rainolds in the ensuing discussion disclaims being a schismatic; "which occasioned a great deal of mirth and raillery between the king and his nobles." After a very long interruption, Rainolds is allowed to proceed. The king interposes as he thinks fit. When Rainolds complains of the circulation of Romish pamphlets by warrant of the Court, James tells him, "Doctor, you are a better collegeman than statesman." Rainolds asks for preaching ministers, which brings Bancroft on his knees again with the petition that all the churches might have "praying ministers," and that all the ministers might be compelled to read the church homilies instead of sermons, because "pulpit harangues are dangerous." The lord-chancellor throws in a remark; the bishop replies with a joke; and the king ends the debate on the point, by promising to "consult the bishops."

When Dr. Rainolds urged his objections to the apocryphal books, the bishops knew not what to say; but the Solomon of the age, as James loved to be called, came to their relief with a torrent of useless learning, closing with the question as he turned to his lords, "What, trow ye, make these men so angry with Ecclesiasticus? By my soul, I think he was a bishop, or they would never use him so." The doctor spoke of the compulsory use of the ceremonies and the vestments. Here James interrupted him with a defence of them in part, and closed by saying, "I will have none of that; I will have one doctrine, one discipline, one religion in substance and ceremony; never speak more to that point, how far you are bound to obey." At length the doctor came to the question of the "prophesyings." The king could contain himself no longer, and instead of hearing the doctor's reasons, he told these intimidated men that he found they were aiming at a Scots Presbytery, "which," says he, "agrees with monarchy as well as God and the devil. Then Jack and Tom, Will and Dick shall meet, and at their pleasure censure both me and my council. Therefore pray stay one seven years before you demand that of me; then if you find me pursy and fat and my windpipe stuffed, I will perhaps hearken to you. But till you find I grow lazy, pray let that alone." Then turning to the bishops he put his hand to his hat and said, "My lords, if once you are out and they in place, I know what would become of my supremacy, for, *no bishop, no king*. Well, doctor, have you any thing else to offer?" "No more," replied the confounded doctor, "if it please your majesty." "Then," said the king, rising from his chair, "if this be all your party have to say, I will make them conform or else I will harry them out of this land, or else worse." And it will appear that he was better than his word; for he harried them *in* the land, and would not let them go out.

Nothing remained but the ceremony, next day, of calling in the Puritans to give them their answer with the closing assurance, "I *will have them enforced* to conformity." Bancroft is in raptures, and again he goes down on his knees. "I protest my heart melteth for joy, that Almighty God, of his singular mercy, hath given us such a king as, since Christ's time, hath not been." And at one point the old archbishop Whitgift, though within six weeks of God's tribunal, is so in transports as to cry out, "Undoubtedly your majesty speaks by the special grace of God."

James chuckles over his exploits upon these frightened doctors. "I soundly peppered off the Puritans," he wrote to a Scotchman, in his exalted way. "They fled me so from argument to argument without ever answering me directly, that I was forced to tell them that if any of them when boys, had disputed thus in college, the moderator would have fetched them up, and applied the rod to their buttocks."

And the bishops and courtiers called James the Solomon of the age. Now for the issue.

## CHAPTER III.

### STAR CHAMBER AND HIGH COMMISSION.

The four doctors in fur gowns have gone home. Fifteen hundred ministers learn the result with disappointment. Many of them are determined they will not submit to the "base, beggarly ceremonies," notwithstanding "the lordly, tyrannous power of the prelates" that enforced them. A stroke of palsy, four weeks later, has silenced the flattering tongue of the old archbishop Whitgift forever; and Bancroft is preparing to take his place. Before Whitgift's body is committed to the tomb, James proclaims to the nation that "his resolutions are unalterably settled," and informs parliament that the Puritans are "an insufferable sect."

And by way of emphasis, ten deputies sent to him with a petition for relief, who found him hunting at the time, are clapped in jail.

James and the bishops go to work in good earnest. The first thing is to get the apparatus of persecution in good working order. One would think that Elizabeth had left little to be desired. There were the Star Chamber and High Commission Courts, with tremendous powers—of which we have more to say presently. There was a fine of twenty pounds a month for staying away from church service—enough to bring poor men pretty surely to jail. There was a requisition, that the ministers all "subscribe" to the church articles and government under penalty of ejection. There was a prohibition of all preaching, catechising, and praying in any private family, where any beside the family were present. The High Commission Court claimed almost unlimited powers of search, arrest and trial

—and of punishment too, whether there were or not any penalties prescribed by the canon law. But all this was not enough.

So at the same time with the parliament, the king called a Convocation or ecclesiastical assembly, and gave them power to make new and sharper canons. Bancroft presided with a will. They very soon turned out a hundred and forty-one canons, that had a grip like a vise. These were immediately ratified by the king's letters patent under the great seal. They ought to have been confirmed by act of parliament to make them bind the laity, as they did the clergy. But the king and the bishops did not concern themselves about that. Let us look at some of the crimes they punished, and see what chance they left for an honest Christian man.

The canons declared that the following persons shall be *excommunicated*—let the reader mark the word, for it meant then not only that a man should be turned out of the congregation of the faithful, and be denied Christian burial when he died, but that he should be rendered *incapable of suing for his lawful debts, and be imprisoned* by civil process *for life*, or until he make satisfaction to the Church—all persons shall be excommunicated who shall affirm either that "the Church of England [with James and Bancroft at its head] is not a true and apostolical church;" or that "its form of worship is corrupt, superstitious or unlawful, or *contains any thing* repugnant to Scripture;" or that "its thirty-nine articles are in any part superstitious or *erroneous*, or such as he may not with a good conscience subscribe to," or that "the rites and ceremonies of the church are wicked, anti-christian, or such as good men may not with a good conscience approve, use, or subscribe;" or that "its government by archbishops, bishops, deans and archdeacons, and the rest that bear office in the same, is anti-christian or repugnant to the Word of God;" or that "the form and manner of making and consecrating bishops, priests or deacons, contain any thing repugnant to the Word of God;"—whosoever "shall separate from the communion of the Church of England and combine together in a new brotherhood;" whosoever shall affirm that ministers separating from the Church of England may "take to themselves the name of another church not established by law, or shall publish that their pretended church has groaned under the burden of certain grievances imposed upon them by the Church of England;" "whosoever shall affirm that there are in this realm other meetings which may rightfully challenge to themselves the name of true and lawful churches;" "whosoever shall affirm that it is lawful for any sort of ministers or lay persons to make rules, orders and constitutions in causes ecclesiastical, without the king's authority, and *shall submit to be governed by them.*"

This is severe enough, certainly. But the Convocation went further; and *cut off the right of appeal* in case of one condemned for these offences, unless he would first recant. They specially re-enjoined all the offensive forms and ceremonies; and required that every preacher should subscribe to the king's supremacy, the prayer book, and the thirty-nine articles, and should declare in the same subscription that he did it *from the heart.* They closed their pleasant work by pronouncing " excommunication " on any man who denied the universal authority of these canons, or aspersed the authority, character and proceedings of the Convocation.

Who could enforce these canons? Many of the very men that made them. The two archbishops and the whole array of bishops, each held his ecclesiastical court—spread thus all over the kingdom—and they could summon and sentence the culprits.

But there was a more terrific body still, called into being by the late Elizabeth and working with fearful energy far into the reign of King James' son Charles—the High Commission Court. It was as absolute as the Inquisition, and its jurisdiction extended over the kingdom. It would summon an accused man, and after he had lain seven weeks in the clink prison, he was brought to trial. The Commissioners put him on oath to *answer all questions* that should be put to him, and then, contrary to the first principles of British law, by a series of searching interrogations, obliged him to accuse himself. If he answered, he was condemned and punished on his own testimony; if he refused, he was imprisoned and punished for contempt of court. This court claimed, and within a dozen years had exercised, the power to deprive men of their estates, to imprison them for life, and even to inflict capital punishment. Its authority embraced offences against the "canons" or church laws. Its spirit was well exhibited about twelve years previously, when Rev. Francis Johnson was before the court. Johnson expressed his surprise that he should be treated in a way which could only make men hypocrites. "Come to the church and obey the queen's laws," was the Commissioner's short reply, "and be a dissembler, a hypocrite or a devil, if thou wilt." Johnson was sent to perpetual banishment.

This court was a terror to the Puritans. If a man wished to bring a minister into trouble, he had only to inform the commissioners by letter that he was a suspected person, and a "pursuivant," or messenger, was sent to his house with a summons. Here we light upon the bishops again; of forty-four commissioners, *twelve were bishops*.

Back of this was another famous, or infamous, tribunal, called the Star Chamber Court—so named because the roof of the room in which it was held was decked with gilt stars. It was an unlawful, but a fearful tribunal; and its members were appointed and removed *by the monarch himself.* Here again our friends the bishops appear; for the court was " made up of certain noblemen, *bishops,* judges and counsellors of the monarch's nomination, to the number of twenty or thirty." It possessed an unlimited discretionary power of fining, imprisoning, banishment, mutilation, and corporal punishment; its jurisdiction extended to all sorts of offences not coming under the cognizance of the ordinary courts; and its proceedings were of the most summary kind. This was the tribunal which in the next reign condemned the lawyer Prynne for writing a book against plays, to have both his ears cut off, to pay a fine of five thousand pounds, (near twenty-five thousand dollars,) and to suffer perpetual imprisonment; and sentenced Dr. Leighton, for an intemperate book against the power of the bishops, to be degraded as a minister, to have his ears cut off, his nose slit, to be branded in the face with a red-hot iron, to stand in the pillory, to be whipped at a post, to pay a fine of a thousand pounds, and to lie in prison till it should be paid—though the parliament afterwards released him at the end of ten years.

To make thorough work, the king summoned this fearful court to the Star Chamber and put to them three questions, to all of which they gave him the answers he wanted. The third question was, "What punishment they deserved *who framed petitions*, and collected *a multitude of hands thereto*, to prefer to the king in a public cause, as the Puritans had done, with an intimation to the king that if he denied their suit, many thousands of his subjects would be discontented?" To which that body replied that this crime of petitioning "was an offence *finable at discretion, and very near to treason and felony* in the punishment."

The king issued his proclamation in July, giving the Puritans till the end of November to conform. Then Bancroft springs to his work. In eleven months he has driven more than three hundred ministers from their places, many of them into prison, and many into foreign lands. Partial concessions were accepted for a time from a multitude of others, only lest the churches should be left destitute.

A heavy hand is that of the bishops. Two Puritans, Mr. Mannsel and Mr. Lad, a minister and a merchant, one Lord's day after sermon, join with Mr. Lackley in repeating the heads of the sermon they had heard in church. Charged with having held a "conventicle," the two former are summoned by the High Commission Court. The oath (to answer all questions put to them) is tendered and refused. They are cast into prison without being admitted to bail. At length they prevail on Nicolas Fuller, an able lawyer, to be their counsel. He moved in court for their discharge on the ground that the High Commissioners were not empowered to commit any of his majesty's subjects to prison. It was an unpardonable offence. Bancroft moved that he be made an example; and Fuller was thrown in prison and kept there till the day of his death.

The ministers that fled from England with their followers, went to various parts of Holland and formed churches, Presbyterian and Independent or Congregational. Many of them were there overwhelmed with poverty. The learned Ainsworth, "a great master of the Oriental languages," lived upon ninepence a week and some boiled roots, hiring himself as porter to a printer, till his employer discovered his skill in the Hebrew language and made it known. Mr. Smyth and his congregation must have gone over about this time.

About the same time, probably, John Robinson was driven from his church near Yarmouth, and soon found his way to Scrooby. But not long could he there find rest. The pursuivants were after him and his friends. Vain were their attempts to elude attention; the eye of the commissioners was on them. Then it was that they resolved to follow their friends to Holland. But it was no easy matter to escape from the country. The king was determined to crush them altogether; and "although they could not stay, yet they were not suffered to go. The ports and havens were shut against them, so that they were fain to seek secret means of conveyance, and to fee the mariners, and give extraordinary rates for their passages. And yet they were oftentimes betrayed, many of them, and both they and their goods intercepted and surprised." Two only of these memorable surprises are recorded. They will be related in the chapter following.

William Brewster and two other members of the Scrooby Church are summoned by the Commissioners of the Province of York to appear on the 22d of April, 1608, at the Collegiate Church of Southwell, some twenty miles from Scrooby. They did not choose to appear. The commissioners imposed a fine of twenty pounds each upon the recusants, and in November made returns to the exchequer to have the fines collected.

If that fine was collected, it was the last that Brewster paid.

## CHAPTER IV.

### BOSTON AND HULL.

FIFTY miles south-east of Scrooby lies the old English seaport, Boston. It is quiet enough now, but there was a time when its business was second only to that of London. Its prosperity, however, had greatly declined in the days of the Pilgrims. It stands on the sluggish river Witham, five miles from the sea, in the midst of a low and marshy region. It possesses one splendid building, the finest parish church in all England, whose lofty tower, two hundred and sixty feet in height, is visible for leagues over the surrounding furs and far away at sea. Two hundred miles directly east across the German Ocean, lies the city of Amsterdam.

One day, in the latter part of the year 1607, William Brewster, William Bradford, and a large company of men, women and children, with their worldly goods, might have been seen upon the way with their faces turned anxiously toward the town that was marked by that lofty tower, which they were now approaching. They were bound for Holland. It was a sore trial to them. They shrunk from leaving " their native country, their lands and livings, and all their friends and familiar acquaintance." That was not all. They were going to a country " where they must learn a new language, and get their livings they knew not how." They thought of Holland as an expensive place to live, involved at that very time in " the miseries of war." They were countrymen and worthy farmers, " not acquainted with trades or traffic," the chief occupations of Holland. Many of them, so they have told us, thought it " an adventure almost desperate, a case intolerable, and a misery worse than death." The only reason why these things "did not dismay them" was that "their desires" (they say) "were set on the ways of God, and to enjoy his ordinances. *They rested on his Providence, and knew whom they had believed.*"

So they "had hired a ship wholly to themselves and made an agreement with the captain to be ready at a certain day, and take them and their goods at a convenient place, where they accordingly would all attend in readiness." They reach Boston— but the captain is not there. "After long waiting and large expenses, he came at length and took them in *at night.*" But better for them if he had not come at all. He is a false-hearted wretch, and has beforehand made secret arrangements with their persecutors. As soon as the company and their goods were all aboard, the officers rushed in. Equally harsh to their victims and faithless to their employers, the officers seem first to have plundered them on their own account. They "put them into open boats and then rifled and ransacked them, searching them to their shirts for money;" nor were "even the women" spared the indecent search. "Their money, books and much" of their other property having been thus taken away, they are carried back into town and "made a spectacle to the multitude who came flocking on all sides to behold them." Among that multitude undoubtedly there were some who in after years came from this very spot and founded another Boston in New England. Thomas Dudley or Richard Bellingham, future governors of Massachusetts, may have been there; or perhaps even a little boy ten years of age, Samuel Whiting, who afterwards was the minister of Lynn. If it had been five years later, John Cotton might have been there—the man who afterwards was preacher in that splendid church, and later yet the famous minister of the second Boston; but that brilliant and eloquent scholar was residing still at Cambridge as one of the Fellows, and soon to be Head Lecturer, of Emanuel College. The exhibition, trying as it was, was not in vain. Here, and afterwards at Hull and Grimsby, "their cause became famous, and occasioned many to look into it." And their Christian deportment "was such as left a deep impression in the minds of many," and afterwards was the means of adding to their numbers.

They are delivered to the magistrates of Boston, and kept under arrest till instructions should come from the lords of the council. The magistrates were friendly and showed them all the favor they could—which is not strange when such a man as the father of Samuel Whiting somewhere about this time was mayor of the city. All of them were confined a month; after which, with the exception of seven principal men, they were dismissed to their homes—if homes they could be said to have. Brewster and six others with him lay still longer in prison and were bound over to the court. Bradford was dismissed earlier on account of his youth.

But though frustrated, they are not shaken in their purpose. The following spring they renew the attempt, but at another place. The little river Idle, that washes Scrooby manor, flows into the Trent, the Trent into the Humber, and the Humber into the German Ocean. On the north bank of the Humber, twenty miles from its mouth, lies the brisk little seaport Hull, and close by the mouth of the river, the ancient but declining port of Grimsby. Distrusting the faith of their countrymen, they seek out a Dutch captain at Hull, state their case to him, gain satisfactory assurances, and make their appointment. To escape observation, they fix upon a solitary place between Grimsby and Hull, where he should meet them, and take them on board. It was a point nearly north from Boston and northeast from Scrooby, about fifty miles distant from each place. The women and children, with the goods, were sent to the appointed spot in a small bark, and the men were to meet them by land. The ship is a day behind them. Meanwhile the sea is rough, and the women sick, and the seamen run the bark into the shelter of a neighboring creek. When the ship arrives next morning, the captain sees the men on shore, and the bark with its contents left fast aground by the ebbing tide—where it must lie till noon. No time is to be lost. A boat is sent for the men on shore. One load of them are on board and the boat is about to return —but, alas! it is too late. The country is roused; a great company of horse and foot are in sight, and rapidly advancing. The

Dutchman, with an oath, weighs anchor and sets sail.

So here are a part of the men on their way to Holland—Bradford among them—with not a change of clothing, and many of them with hardly a penny in their pockets, their wives and children left to the tender mercies of their persecutors. They could not restrain their tears; they would have given all they had " to be again on shore ;" but there was no remedy. And soon it became a question whether those wives and children would ever see them more. A fearful storm fell on them and tossed them about for fourteen days, during which they were driven upon the coast of Norway and for a whole week saw neither sun, moon nor stars. The sailors " with cries and shrieks" gave up all hope; the passengers " without any great distraction" gave themselves to fervent prayer, and " with a great height of divine faith cried, 'Yet, Lord, thou canst save; yet, Lord, thou canst save.'" When they reached the port in safety, they felt it to be in answer to their prayers.

Of the men who were left behind, those who were needed to assist the women, remained; the rest made their escape. But bitter was the distress of the company in the bark, and sad the sight they presented—children "hanging about" their mothers, "crying for fear, and quaking with cold, and the mothers themselves in deep distress, weeping on every side for their husbands that were carried away," for "the poor little ones hanging about them," for their forlorn and miserable prospects, "not knowing what should become of them and their little ones," as they "had no homes to go to." The magistrates were sadly at a loss what to do with them. "To imprison so many women and innocent children for no other cause but that they would go with their husbands seemed unreasonable;" "and to send them to their homes again was as difficult, for they had sold their houses and livings." So they "harried them round" from one place to another, and from one justice to another, till all were wearied and tired with them and glad to be rid of them on any terms. In the meantime "the poor souls endured misery enough."

But the wise and cheerful Brewster and the calm and beloved Robinson remained with them in England through all their troubles. Retreat could not now be thought of; a necessity lay upon them to go, and it "forced a way for them"—for most likely the magistrates found it indispensable to let them go. "In the end, notwithstanding these storms of opposition, they all got over, some at one time and some at another, and met together again, according to their desires, with no small rejoicing." Rejoicing, indeed! when those anxious husbands and fathers, those forlorn and weeping wives, and those affrighted, homeless children rushed to each other's arms! Robinson and Brewster, who had "stayed to help the weakest over before them," came with the last company; and all are together again, but in a foreign land.

These trials had been hard for them, but not without their uses for the Master's cause. Their faith, and constancy, and Christian deportment, and their purpose, too, had been thoroughly advertised in these three important places, Boston, Hull and Grimsby, and in the region round about. They made their mark. And it is noticeable how when in later days they found their way across the Atlantic no portion of the mother country was so abundantly represented in the emigration that followed them, as the region round about the scene of their sufferings and notoriety. The name of Boston itself and of a score or two of towns lying within a radius of sixty or eighty miles

—Hull, Waltham, Cambridge, Beverly, Hingham, Needham, Framingham, Ashby, Yarmouth, Braintree, Lynn, Boxford, Sudbury, Ipswich, Haverhill, Woburn, Leicester, Northampton, Hatfield, Wenham, and others—transferred to the earlier settlements of Massachusetts, bear witness to the origin of many of the early colonists themselves. Little but the pure gold, too, could pass through such a fire.

Those despairing women and those anxious men saw not fully the reason for their trials. But God had a reason, nevertheless.

## CHAPTER V.

### HOLLAND.

The Pilgrims are safe at last in Holland. Why are they here? They came because here they could find perfect safety; and God brought them here, apparently to teach them some lessons they could not have learned, had not their way to Plymouth led through Holland. Here was "a church without a bishop and a state without a king." Here was the only state in Europe or the world, where there was then perfect civil tolerance on religious subjects. God sent the pioneers of New England thither to make them more thoroughly tolerant and republican than any other band of emigrants that came to America. As they were to shape the whole history of New England, they were made to undergo a severer training, and a more thorough maturing, and to gain wiser and more liberal views by a broader experience. In after days they refrained from some of the practical errors of the later colonists. And though comparatively few and poor, their early influence on the first settlement of New England was invaluable. How came the state of things they found in Holland?

It was the fruit of one of the most terrible histories of suffering that the annals of the world contain. The fierce and murky elements that kept the heavens of England in commotion for more than a hundred years, with successive storms of persecution, with lowering clouds and muttering thunders and flashing fires, had swept through Holland in one long and awful hurricane, and burned themselves out at last, to leave the sky all bright and pure.

In England, the movement of the Reformation had been slow. Three-quarters of a century had passed already since Henry VIII., the great-great-uncle of James the First, had rudely torn England from the authority of the pope, because the pope refused to grant him a divorce from Catharine, his queen. But Henry, having broken away from Rome, suppressed the monasteries and absorbed their wealth, afterward endeavored to hold the English Reformation where it was. He withdrew the permission, once given, to read the Word of God, retained auricular confession, the seven sacraments, the celibacy of the clergy, the doctrine of transubstantiation, prayers for the dead, invocation of the saints, and most of the peculiarities of popery, except the supreme authority of the pope. And so he held the kingdom in an ambiguous condition, wherein he continued to burn as heretics those who avowed the doctrines of

Luther, and to **hang as** traitors those who maintained the supremacy **of** the pope. Indeed on one occasion, in 1540, three Protestant ministers and four Papists were sent on the same hurdle or **cart** to the same place **of** execution. In **the** brief reign **of** Henry's son, Edward VI., Protestantism was made the national religion, the prayer-book compiled from the Romish missals, and thus from the ancient liturgies, substantially, into its present form, and a higher pitch of liberality attained in one respect than ever since in the Episcopal Church, namely, in recognizing foreign churches without bishops, and foreign ministers not ordained by bishops, as true churches and ministers. But persecution continued to some extent towards those who went beyond a certain range; Anabaptists were burned. Then came bloody Queen Mary, another of Henry's children, to re-establish Romanism. In her reign of about five years and **a** half, besides those who were secretly murdered in prison, *four hundred persons*, including sixty women and forty little children, *were burned alive* for their religion. There is a place in London, called Smithfield, now used for a cattle market, rich with the blood of the martyrs. Those fires of Smithfield began with good John Rogers, the man who at the stake refused to recant for an offered pardon, though a wife and ten children bound him to the world. The reign of Elizabeth, though not so polluted with blood, was severe on non-conformity. By the act of uniformity, passed in the second year of her reign, any minister who should venture to address his Maker in other language than that of the Book of Common Prayer, was liable to the loss of goods and chattels for the first offence, to twelve months' imprisonment for the second, and imprisonment during life for the third. It was she who established the High Commission Court.

The Anabaptists still were executed; Barrow, Greenwood and Penry suffered death, and the members of the Southwark Church lay in prison; and others fled the country. Then came James, to be followed by the heavy hand of Charles with his notorious Archbishop Laud. Never for an hour was the principle of full toleration erected in England till the glorious government of Cromwell—then to be long again submerged.

But in Holland the state of things had long been different. The terrific struggle for liberty of conscience had been carried through in the reigns of the famous Emperor Charles the Fifth and his fanatical son Philip II., of Spain; and a quarter of a century before the death of Philip, William the Silent, Prince of Orange, had founded the Dutch Republic on principles of full toleration.

The train of events may be briefly sketched. The Reformation had swept into Holland almost immediately on the public appearance of Luther,—the provinces of Holland being the paternal inheritance of the Emperor Charles. It was the one deep regret of Charles' latest hours, that when Luther appeared before him at the celebrated Diet of Worms, he had not violated his own royal word and sign-manual and put Luther to death! But he showed his disposition. For in that very year, 1521, and from the very place of the Diet, the young emperor had issued an arbitrary edict for Holland, declaring that as " the aforesaid Martin [Luther] is not a man, but a devil under the form of a man, and clothed in the dress of a priest, the better to bring the human race to hell and damnation, therefore *all his disciples are to be punished with death and confiscation of goods.*" Another edict soon forbade *all private assemblies for devotion; all reading of the Scriptures; all discussions within one's own doors* concerning faith, the sacraments, the papal authority, or other religious matters, *under penalty of death.* Then, in 1535, come still another edict condemning all heretics, whether repentant or persevering, to death; repentant males to be executed with the sword, repentant females to be buried alive; the obstinate of both sexes to be burned. These horrible edicts were all re-enacted in a body by subsequent decrees, and remained the law of the land throughout the reign of Charles.

To do this bloody work, Charles introduced the Inquisition into Holland, and appointed his sister, Mary, Dowager Queen of Hungary, Regent of the Netherlands. This woman, worthy to be, as both she and the emperor were, first cousin to bloody Mary of England, wrote to her brother in 1533, that in her opinion "all heretics, whether repentant or not, should be persecuted with such severity that error might be at once extinguished, care being only taken that the provinces *were not entirely depopulated.*" The awful work was thoroughly done. The number of Hollanders who, during the reign of Charles and in obedience to his edicts, had been beheaded, burned and buried alive for the offences above enumerated, swelled to the dreadful total of one hundred thousand!

Charles resigned his dominions at last to his son Philip, charging him, as one of his last injunctions, to maintain the Catholic religion; then retired to his monastery at Juste to issue savage exhortations to his son to cut out the root of heresy.

Philip the Second needed no exhortations. He had been well mated when he married "bloody Mary." He gave himself to "the rooting out of heresy," and the maintenance of Romanism, as the work to which his life was consecrated; and more than once expressed the willingness to sacrifice all his dominions, if need were, in the effort. Full of cunning yet destitute of wisdom, hesitating and yet obstinate, more utterly devoid of truth and honor than it is possible for language to set forth—so did he make his whole life an atmosphere of lying—bitter and relentless, yea, never yet cleared of deep suspicions concerning the murder of his eldest son. Philip devoted his earliest leisure to carry out the purpose of his life. In 1559 he appointed his sister, the duchess of Parma, Regent of the country; and being about to withdraw into Spain, he solemnly charged her in public thoroughly to *enforce the edicts and decrees* made by the Emperor Charles, and now renewed by Philip himself, for the extirpation of all sects and heresies. The monarch celebrated his arrival in Spain with a splendid *auto da fe*, in which he feasted his eyes with the sight of thirteen distinguished victims burning at the stake.

Already the reformed religion had gained a strong foothold in Holland, coming in through the Lutheranism of Germany on one side, and the Calvinism of France on the other. The edict which Philip re-enacted and left as his parting gift to Holland inflicted its terrible penalty on those who should print, write, copy, keep, conceal, buy, sell or give any book or writing composed by Calvin, Luther, Zwingle, and other heretics—those who should injure images of the virgin or the saints—those who should be present at any Protestant meetings—all lay persons who should read, teach, or dispute concerning the Holy Scriptures, openly or secretly—those who should *entertain any of the opinions* of Luther, Calvin, &c. The penalty was burning alive, and forfeiture of all the property. If they repented, the men might receive the mercy of being executed with the sword, the women of being buried alive. Any person harboring or supplying a suspected heretic, or failing to denounce him, should receive the heretic's doom. A bounty was offered to the informer; and the traitor who should attend a " conventicle " and then betray his friends, should receive a full pardon.

Spanish soldiery were left, and new bishops appointed in Holland, to aid in executing the destined work. Peter Titelman and a dozen other inquisitors sprang eagerly to their calling. The prisons swarmed with victims, and the streets with processions to the stake. Occasionally the dull routine of strangling, burning and burying alive, was relieved by some such case as that of Bertrand le Blas, who had snatched a consecrated wafer from the priest, and with the exclamation, " Misguided men, do you deem this thing to be Jesus Christ your Lord and Saviour?" had broken it to fragments, and trampled it on the ground. This man was thrice put to the torture. He was dragged, on a hurdle, with his mouth closed with an iron gag, to the market place. His right hand and foot were burned and twisted off between two red-hot irons—his tongue torn out by the roots, and the iron gag again applied. With his arms and legs fastened together behind his back, he was then fastened by the middle of his body to an iron chain, and swung back and forth over a slow fire till he was roasted.

Sometimes a whole family were taken off; thus John de Swarte, his wife and four children were all burned together. Secret drowning was substituted, to some extent, for public burning, to take away the glory of the martyr's death. And so the work went on. Still the inquisitors complained of delay. Philip urged from Spain. At length the phrenzy of the people was aroused. Religious assemblies met every where under arms—and field preaching spread in all directions. Pledges of resistance began to be made throughout the provinces, and confederations formed. The great religious assemblies—or camp-meetings—where the worshipers came all armed to the teeth, sometimes numbered fifteen or even twenty thousand persons. A fierce popular outbreak rose in Antwerp, and in a single night the magnificent cathedral, whose spire rose five hundred feet, and whose interior was adorned with the most gorgeous and costly decorations—a maze of art and wealth—was completely disemboweled of its images, its relics, and all its treasures, and made a wreck within. The affrighted Regent was about to fly from the country, and was with difficulty restrained. The Protestants obtained permission from the terrified government to hold their religious assemblies unmolested, till advice should be received from the king. Envoys are sent to Spain, asking the abolition of the inquisition, revocation of the edicts, and pardon of offenders. Philip dissembled, and meditated meanwhile the most awful vengeance.

At length all was ready. An armed invasion of Holland is resolved upon; and ten thousand chosen and veteran Spanish soldiers are detached under the command of the duke of Alva. The name of this man has come down to us laden with infamy. He was the ablest general in Europe, and was sixty years of age. Cruel, unscrupulous and indifferent to public opinion, he was in every respect a fit instrument to execute the designs of Philip.

One can almost see that cast-iron man, "tall, thin, erect, with a small head, a long visage, lean, yellow cheek, dark, twinkling eyes, adust complexion, black, bristling hair, and long, sable-silvered beard," as he marches on his track of perfidy and blood;

and that veteran army, accompanied by a corps of *two thousand prostitutes*, regularly enrolled and distributed as part of the equipment, as it wound on its way to butcher, burn and ravish for the sake of the "holy Catholic religion."

No resistance at first was offered. The cities of Holland surrendered their keys. Two chief nobles of Holland, Counts Egmont and Horn, trusting the lying assurances of Alva and his master Philip, are decoyed within Alva's grasp, and he passes his arm lovingly over the neck of Egmont, already devoted to the block. In a few days they are hurried from the banquet to the prison, and soon after their headless bodies lay on the scaffold in the great square of Brussels. The execution of eighteen other prisoners of distinction had just preceded; and long before their tragic end the streams of blood had been pouring forth like water.

Alva had established a court superseding

all other tribunals, to be known in history, forever, as the Blood Council. This court, in horribly sweeping terms, pronounced guilty of treason, all who had ever signed a petition against the new bishops, the inquisition or the edicts; all who had under any circumstances tolerated public preaching; those who had ever omitted resistance to the field preaching, the image-breaking, the presentation of a remonstrance by the nobles; or who should have asserted that the king did not possess the right to deprive all the provinces of their liberties, or who should have maintained that this court—utterly illegal though it was—was bound in any manner to respect any laws and charters;— and the punishment of treason was pronounced to be instant death. The method of the court was as summary as its character was arbitrary. Its examination of evidence was the merest mockery, and individuals arrested for trial were not seldom executed before their names were reached. Nothing in modern history, but the Revolutionary Tribunal in France, two hundred years later, will compare with it. In three months it had destroyed eighteen hundred lives, and was just entering on its work. Men were sentenced by platoons. In a single day, for example, eighty-four inhabitants of Valenciennes were condemned; on another day forty-six inhabitants of Malines; on another, ninety-five from different parts of Flanders. A grand swoop was made on the holiday of Shrovetide, and five hundred victims caught and executed. Anguish was carried into every village and almost every family in the land. Alva told the deputies of Antwerp that "his majesty would rather the whole land should become an uninhabited wilderness, than that a single dissenter should exist within its territory."

It seemed as though this threat was to be made good. In February, 1568, a decree of the inquisition pronounced *sentence of death on all the inhabitants of the Netherlands, as heretics.* From this sentence of death on three millions of men, women and children, only a few persons, especially named, were excepted. The king's proclamation confirmed the sentence, and ordered its execution. The intention, of course, was not actually to slaughter all, but to give complete facility for the destruction of any. The Blood Council wrought the harder. The solemnities of Holy Week were followed by the fall of eight hundred heads. To avoid all disturbance as the victims marched through the streets on such occasions, they were gagged by having the tongue thrust through an iron ring, and then seared by a hot iron and thus made fast. It were a mere harrowing of the feelings further to detail these proceedings. Enough that when Alva resigned his command of six years' duration, he boasted that *eighteen thousand and six hundred persons* had been sent by him to *execution* alone,—besides the countless victims who had been slaughtered in his military murders. More than a hundred thousand men abandoned their country.

Just about this time the noble Baron Montigny, who had left his young four-months bride to go as ambassador to Spain, and had lain there four years in confinement, was secretly strangled in prison. All the complicated details of his private murder, were arranged minutely by king Philip with a man of awful perfidy and falsehood, now revealed after the lapse of three centuries, which almost staggers belief.

The noble Prince of Orange rallied his countrymen to resistance. Ill-supplied and feebly supported, some opening successes were followed by bitter reverses; and the Hollanders abandoned the struggle. Fresh slaughters succeeded. In the infatuation of his victories. Alva imposed the most exhausting and even ruinous taxes on the wealth and trade of Holland. All business was arrested. The people stood appalled, and feeling at length their forlorn and desperate condition, **again set** up the standard of revolt. **The** Prince of Orange, who from **an** outward Catholic, had been led along until **he** became not only **a** Protestant, but a deeply religious man, with an unfaltering trust in God amid reverses and ingratitude, and sometimes beggary and desertion, like **a** very father of his country, led **the** nation. From the beginning of his mission in 1572, he proclaimed *perfect freedom to religion*, under penalty of death **to** those who infringed it.

Hardly had success and hope began to crown his struggles, when he was thunderstruck and deep gloom was cast upon his prospects by the "massacre of Saint Bartholomew." The neighboring monarch,

Charles IX., of France, who had pledged him aid, gave from his royal palace the signal of that havoc, and from his palace window, with gun in hand, shot at his subjects; and within thirty days the blood of unknown thousands of Protestants (from 25,000 to 100,000) watered the streets of Paris and the villages of France. The pope of Rome in grand procession with his cardinals, went to the church of St. Mark to render thanks to God for this signal grace; Philip of Spain congratulated the monarch of France not only for the valorous exploit, but for an event to which "he owed the preservation of the Netherlands." Alva is stimulated, his victims disheartened. Why detail the awful scenes that marked the taking of such places as Zutphen and Naarden, when in the former place the orders were to spare not a single man alive, nor leave a house unburned, and where the citizens were stabbed, or hung upon their own shade trees, or stripped naked and turned into the fields to freeze in the wintery nights, or hung by *the feet* upon the gallows to be four days and nights in perishing,—and, at last, five hundred of them tied two and two, back to back, and drowned in the river Yssel; and in the latter place, beside all other conceivable horrors carried on with shouts of laughter as a wild amusement, the soldiers even in some cases drank the blood from their victims' veins. And both here and in every place which the Spaniards took, the women were surrendered to the worst outrages that could be inflicted on them.

Such scenes as these marked their path, and the pen is weary to record over and over these same dreadful outrages. Throughout this whole career, " men were tortured, beheaded, hanged by the neck and legs, burned before slow fires, pinched to death with red-hot tongs, broken on the wheel, starved, and flayed alive. Their skins stripped from the living body, were stretched upon drums, to be beaten in the march of their brethren to the gallows."

Still the patriots rallied nobly. There was the long and desperate defence of Harlem, in which even a military company of women did noble service, and in which an army of 30,000 besiegers left 12,000 of their number dead around the city, before the absolutely starving inhabitants surrendered. There was the siege of Alkmaar, in which eight hundred soldiers and thirteen hundred citizens, resisted sixteen thousand Spanish troops and in three terrible assaults were driven back, while every living man was on the walls; and not alone cannon balls and bullets, but boiling water, pitch and oil, melted lead, tarred and burning hoops, were hurled forth, and amid the flying missiles, undaunted women and children passed back and forth with powder and ball for their fathers and brothers, until even some of the

Spanish soldiers suffered themselves to be run through the body rather than again advance to the walls; and their commander learning that the Prince of Orange had already given orders to cut down the dykes and let the waters of the ocean flood the land, called off his fiends of war. Every thing, indeed, was at stake for Alkmaar; for Alva had privately declared that he "would not leave a single creature alive."

Alva at length, laden with crime and detestation was permitted to retire. His successor made from time to time some show of reconciliation; but the attempt at subjugation still went on. Philip's purpose was not to be shaken. The struggle continued, marked by various successes and many reverses too. One of the most gallant things in history was the long and triumphant defence of Leyden. One of the most awful chapters in the annals of military crime was the sacking of Antwerp, still known as "the Spanish Fury"—in which every conceivable atrocity ran riot, and eight thousand citizens were slaughtered, six millions of property destroyed by fire, and at least six millions more were carried off by the Spaniards. More desperate, resolute, and united grew the resistance of Holland. Often defeated, never despairing, always trusting in the God to whom he committed all, Orange finally came off victorious.

In a time of his deepest discouragement and destitution of all foreign help, he replied to the despondent inquiry of one of his advisers: "You ask if I have entered into a firm treaty with any great king or potentate, to which I answer, that before I ever took up the cause of the oppressed Christians in these provinces, I had entered into a close alliance with the King of kings; and I am firmly convinced that all who put their trust in Him, shall be saved by His almighty hand. The God of armies will raise up armies for us to do battle with our enemies and His own." And the God of armies did remember him. The interpositions of Heaven seemed quite as remarkable, and as indispensable too, as in our own Revolutionary war.

Seven provinces formed the Republic of the United Netherlands. Met by the Spanish commanders with alternate attempts at bribery and assassination, the Prince of Orange fell at length by the assassin's hand in 1584. His son and successor, Maurice, followed in his steps with a constant succession of battles, sieges and victories, till at length the peace of Antwerp, formed in the very year after the arrival of the Pilgrims, gave a twelve years' breathing spell to the harassed land.

But for many years before the establishment of peace, Holland became the refuge of the persecuted in all parts of Europe. Thousands expelled by Spanish cruelty from

Southern Netherlands, (now Belgium,) Huguenots from France, and Puritans from England, flocked into the Northern Netherlands, now Holland. At Rotterdam, the Hague, Leyden, Utrecht, and other places, there were English churches formed on the Presbyterian plan, as well as those of Episcopal government.

The great and flourishing city of Amsterdam especially was a point of attraction. For fifteen years already, when the Pilgrims arrived, there had been an Independent Puritan Church in Amsterdam, and another was formed just before their arrival. Among these were many of the men who had lain in the prisons of London, when Barrowe and Greenwood and Penry were summoned forth to the scaffold. The court and the bishops in England, after the execution of Penry, staggered by the odium of executing for treason men who died with the strongest expressions of loyalty on their lips, had cleared the prisons of them by sentence of banishment. And here they had long been in Amsterdam, with their pastors, Francis Johnson and Henry Ainsworth. There were more than three hundred communicants in the older church at Amsterdam.

## CHAPTER VI.

### LEYDEN.

The pilgrims landed in Amsterdam. Brewster may perhaps have been there when he was in Holland, more than twenty years before. Even to his eyes it must have been greatly changed; trade and wealth had flowed in, until the city was almost three times as large as then. To the other members of the little band it was a strange sight, "all so far differing," they say, "from their plain country villages, wherein they were bred and had so long lived, that it seemed they were come into a new world." The wealth and luxury that revelled around, only stood in stronger contrast with their own destitution and almost beggary. Hear their sad and yet manly reminiscence: "Though they saw fair and beautiful cities, flowing with abundance of all sorts of wealth and riches, yet it was not long before they saw the grim and grisly face of poverty coming upon them like an armed man, with whom they must buckle and encounter, and from whom they could not fly. But they were armed with faith and patience against him and all his encounters; and though they were sometimes foiled, yet by God's assistance they prevailed and got the victory." In truth, with the exception of a very few persons, like Brewster and Bradford, they were originally men of small means, and what little they possessed had been pretty thoroughly stripped away in the hardships of their removal. Even Brewster was now reduced like the rest. And the difficulty was for men who had been brought up in agricultural occupations, to maintain themselves in a country that depended so largely on its trade and manufactures.

But they did not remain long in Amsterdam. For the sake of their religious peace, these tempest-tossed men were willing to make another removal within a year, "though they well knew," so they say, "it would be much to the prejudice of their outward estates, both at the present and in the future." They found the independent churches at Amsterdam in the midst of a contention, with the strongest prospect of its increase rather than its diminution. It is the misfortune of all human movements, however good, often to be discredited by a few unworthy individuals. The better the cause and the more of courage and zeal it requires, the greater the liability to be weighed down by individuals who possess "zeal without knowledge," and who push that zeal beyond all the bounds of wisdom, reason and charity. So the Pilgrims found it to be in

Amsterdam. The church itself was a miscellaneous collection; and three sources of trouble had sprung up. Mr. John Smyth had led off a secession church, upon a singular mixture of Baptist and Perfectionist principles, with certain fanatical doctrines, such as that flight in time of persecution was unlawful, and the singing of set words or verses to God was unauthorized. In the original church trouble had arisen about a case of discipline, which grew out of certain excessive views upon the plainness of female dress. And finally, one of the pastors of that church, Mr. Johnson, advocated Presbyterian views of church government, while Mr. Ainsworth and the bulk of the church were Congregational. In view of the present and the coming troubles, Robinson and his church determined to remove "before they were engaged" in them.

Leyden became their home in Holland. And though "not so beneficial to their outward means of living" as Amsterdam, no place was invested with more befitting associations for such a band. It was but about thirty years since the city had braved and vanquished still more terrific foes than theirs. One of the noblest defences in the records of history was made at Leyden. In 1574, after a blockade of five months, and while scantily supplied and almost without troops, the city was invested by the Spanish army, and girdled with sixty-two redoubts so effectually that scarcely any thing but a carrier-pigeon could find its way out or in. The citizens felt, as did the Prince of Orange, that the fate of the country hinged on their manhood, and girded themselves solemnly and resolutely to the work of resistance. The food which they had early weighed out on allowance, soon failed. The flesh of horses, dogs and rats, weeds and every substance by which human life can be protracted, were eaten and exhausted. One only hope remained—to break down the dykes and sluices and let the ocean drive out their invaders. To this appalling desolation of a vast territory, the consent of the States of Holland was asked—and given. "Better a drowned land," said they, "than a lost land." The dykes were opened, but a contrary wind long kept back the waters. Starvation began. Anxious messages were sent to the Prince to hasten the relief; but, alas! broken down with his overwhelming cares, a raging fever was coursing through his veins. Day after day they mounted the ancient tower and looked despairingly towards the ocean, fifteen miles away. The enemy taunted them. Once, indeed, a band of the more faint-hearted citizens thronged the house of their burgomaster and demanded a surrender. "I tell you," replied the haggard but undaunted man, "I have made an oath to hold the city, and may God give me strength to keep my oath! I can die but once. . . . I know that we shall starve if not soon relieved; but starvation is better than the dishonored death which is the only alternative. Take my body to appease your hunger, but expect no surrender from me." They catch the flame—return to the walls—and hurl new defiance to the enemy. "Ye call us rat-eaters and dog-eaters; and it is true. So long, then, as ye hear dog bark, or cat mew, within these walls, ye may know that the city holds out. And when all has perished but ourselves, be sure that we will each eat our left arms, retaining our right to defend our women, our liberty, and our religion, against the foreign tyrant."

At length Orange recovered. A violent gale from the north-west piled up the waters of the ocean in huge masses, and sent them pouring through the broken dykes. The whole country around Leyden became a vast lake, over which those anxious eyes soon saw the fleet of Orange approaching to their relief. From one chief fortress the Spaniards fled in terror along the dykes and causeways, and were drowned and slain as they went. That night the remainder of the besieging army disappeared in silence. In the morning the famished citizens rushed with frantic eagerness to meet their deliverers and their food. Then they marched in solemn procession to the great church to give thanks to God. Prayer was offered; and thousands of voices lifted the song of praise, but broke down with an uncontrollable weeping. Six thousand of their dear friends had died of starvation.

Among the privileges bestowed on the city for its heroic defence, was the foundation of the University of Leyden. Five months only from the close of the siege the city was all astir with the inauguration ceremonies. The University soon became famous, and has been adorned with many names of European reputation. Such names as these, Grotius, Descartes, Scaliger and Boerhaave, are found in the list of its professors; and the city itself was called the Athens of the West, and the North Star of Holland.

To Leyden came the Pilgrims, "valuing peace and their spiritual comfort," says Bradford, "above any other riches whatsoever; and at length they came to raise a comfortable living with hard and continual labor." Bradford himself learned the art of silk-dyeing. Brewster taught Dutch students the English language, and after a time became quite popular as a teacher. And toward the latter portion of the residence in Leyden he set up a printing-press and issued several religious books that were prohibited in England, till at length the British government again set its watchful eye upon him, and reached out its long arm after him. He was thought to be arrested once; but the drunken officer had seized the wrong man. He was followed so close, however, that during the last year which the company spent in Holland, Brewster and his family, with all their goods, were lying snugly concealed in England, probably in London, where it is thought he kept close till the Mayflower sailed. Others of the expatriated band were weavers, who made a living by their looms, which they carried with them.

Thus they resorted to every lawful device for a subsistence. They succeeded—but by the hardest labor. It was "great labor and hard fare," and "it was low with many of them." Their admirable and Christian traits helped them not a little. "When they wanted money their word would be taken amongst the Dutch, because they had found by experience how careful they were to keep their word, and saw them so painful [pains-taking] and diligent in their callings." The preference was even given to them in their labors, and their custom was sought by the tradesmen, " for their honesty and diligence." So unexceptionable was their deportment, that not long before their departure, the magistrates in public court bore honorable testimony to them: " These English," said they to the Walloons of the French Church, " have lived among us now this twelve years, and yet we have never had any suit or accusation come against any of them. But *your* strifes are continual." Mr. Robinson their pastor—for Mr. Clifton had remained at Amsterdam—was soon recognized as a rare man, and treated with much consideration. It so happened that the two Divinity Professors in the University, Episcopius and Polyander, became engaged in a warm controversy on what is called Arminianism—Arminius himself having been a professor in the University, and died on the year of Robinson's arrival. Episcopius was an Arminian, Polyander a Calvinist. Robinson, of course, held with the latter; and, by his earnest and pressing solicitation, three times appeared in discussion against Episcopius. And, says Bradford, "the Lord did so help him to defend the truth and foil his adversary that he put him to an apparent non-plus in this great and public audience." It has been suggested that this claiming of the victory may be the result of friendly partiality. But whether this be so or not, Robinson's published works show him to have been a man of rare abilities; and it is clear that in Leyden his estimation was high. After six years' residence he was received as a member of the University—a privilege attended with the rather singular benefits of exempting him from the control of the town magistrates, and entitling him to half a tun of beer every month, and about ten gallons of wine every three months—if he chose to receive them. And when at length he died, five years after the sailing of the Mayflower and the Speedwell, the " magistrates, ministers, scholars and most of the gentry of Leyden mourned his death as a public loss, and followed him to the grave."

Here " they continued many years in a comfortable condition, enjoying much sweet and delightful society and spiritual comfort together, in the ways of God, under the able ministry and prudent government of Mr. John Robinson and Mr. William Brewster, who was an assistant unto him in the place of an elder, unto which he was now called and chosen by the church ; so that they grew in knowledge and other gifts and graces of the Spirit of God; and lived together in peace, and love, and holiness." And the same writer who makes this statement, and who himself was there from the beginning to the end, adds a testimony which need not be disputed : " I know not but that it may be spoken to the honor of God, and without prejudice to any, that such was the humble zeal and fervent love of this people towards God and his ways, and the single-heartedness and sincere affection one towards another, that they came as near the primitive pattern of the first churches as any other church of these latter times has done, according to their rank and quality."

Meanwhile many persons from various parts of England joined them, until their number amounted at last to more than three hundred persons. Here they were joined by the good soldier, afterwards their military chief in America, Myles Standish. He had served among the English troops sent by Queen Elizabeth to aid the Hollanders in their struggles for liberty; and encountering the Pilgrims at Leyden, cast in his lot with theirs. The town of Duxbury, in Massachusetts, where he afterwards had his home and laid his bones to rest, commemorates his recollections of the English Duxbury, his earlier home, where the family name of Standish is still perpetuated in one of the oldest families of Lancashire. Edward Winslow, twenty-two years old, traveling on the continent with his wife, arrived at Leyden and joined them too—afterwards their governor in Plymouth. Here, probably, John Carver, one of their deacons and the first of their governors, found them.

During their residence here, their views were liberalized towards men of other true Christian churches; and they were displaying that spirit of broad charity which has commonly marked the congregational churches in later times. Robinson had been "more rigid in his course at first than towards his latter end." But it was their practice freely to commune with the French and the Dutch churches; they invited a Scotch Presbyterian minister to their communion table in Leyden, though the invitation was for prudential reasons, declined. And in regard to the English Church, Robinson "advised us by all means to endeavor to close with the godly party of the kingdom of England, and rather to study union than division." And while they objected to the "mixed communion" of Christians and impenitent men together, and condemned the government of that church by bishops and a monarch as unscriptural, and therefore denied the National Church, as *national*, to be a true church; they never objected to listening to the preaching of the evangelical ministers of that church, nor to communing with them and their godly communicants separate from the whole congregation; and they have left on record the statement that "there are [in that church] some parish assemblies that are true churches, by virtue of an implicit covenant among themselves, in which regard the Church of England may be held and called a true church."*

But they cannot remain here. Robinson and Brewster have been anxiously looking at their condition, and feel that they are not accomplishing their best usefulness. They lay their views before various brethren, proposing another removal. From "private discussion" it passes to "public agitation;" and "the congregation, with fasting and prayer, seek the Lord to direct us." Objections are made, "many fears and doubts" are expressed.

Robinson and Brewster, "with some of the sagest members," urge these reasons: First, they are shut up from all prospect of growth. It is so difficult to maintain themselves that few persons joined them, and some who came could not stay. Surrounded on all sides by foreigners, they are afraid

---

* Bradford's Dialogue, in Young's Chronicles of the Pilgrims, p. 416.

they may even lose the English language in process of time. Secondly, the original stock of emigrants are growing old and wearing out with " their great and continual labors;" and there is danger that the whole enterprise should eventually fade away. Thirdly, they are inexpressibly anxious for their children. " We were unable to give such education to our children as we ourselves had received." Nay, their sons and daughters, were " oppressed with the weight of their labors, and became decrepit in early youth, the vigor of nature being consumed in the very bud." But worst of all, and " of all sorrows most heavy to be borne," those children were in danger of becoming morally " degenerate and corrupted." The Holy Sabbath, which they were accustomed to reverence, was then, as now upon the continent of Europe, constantly profaned on every hand around. Their sons driven by the pressure within, and drawn by the temptations without, were breaking away from parental control; some went to sea, some joined the army, and others fell into courses tending still more "to the great grief of their parents and the dishonor of God." A last and apparently the greatest reason was their burning desire to spread the gospel "in the remote parts of the world." Apparently their isolated condition forced upon them the conviction that they were in a measure wasting their influence and living only for themselves, when there was much work to do for the kingdom of Christ. And they had thought of America as the place of their labors.

These things they urge on their brethren. There are some to urge strong counter reasons. It was a design attended with "many inconceivable perils." There are "the casualties of the seas," and "the length of the voyage," such as the aged and the feeble "could never endure," the "miseries of the land," "liable to famine, nakedness and the want of all things," with probability of disease from the "change of air, diet and water;" "continual danger of the savage people, cruel, barbarous and treacherous, not content only to kill, but flaying men alive with the shells of fishes, cutting off the joints and members and broiling them on coals, and causing men to eat the collops of flesh in their sight; with other cruelties too horrible to be related." Then where was the money to come from, for the transportation; where the supplies to sustain them on their arrival? Others had lamentably failed in the attempt. They themselves had found it hard enough to arrive in Holland and live even in that rich and well-regulated commonwealth. How would it be in the wilderness beyond the broad ocean?

All these objections were urged; and weighty ones they were. No wonder they "moved the bowels of men to grate within them," and made " the weak to quake and tremble." But Robinson and his friends answered by frankly admitting the difficulties, and asserting the need of a corresponding courage. "The dangers," said they, " are great, but not desperate, and the difficulties many, but not invincible; for although many of them are likely, yet they are not certain. It may be that some of the things feared may never befall us; others by providence, care, and the use of good means, may in a great measure be prevented; and all of them through the help of God, by fortitude and patience may be either borne or overcome. True it is that such attempts are not to be made and undertaken but upon good ground and reason, not rashly or lightly, as many have done for curiosity or hope of gain. But our condition here is not ordinary. Our ends are good and honorable, our calling lawful and urgent; and therefore we may expect the blessing of God in our proceeding. Yea, though *we should lose our lives in this action, yet we may have comfort in so doing;* and our *endeavors* will be honorable. We live here as men in exile and in a poor condition, and as great miseries may possibly befall us in this place ; for the twelve years truce are out and there is nothing but beating of drums and preparing for war, the events of which are always uncertain. The Spaniard may prove as cruel as the savages of America; and the famine and pestilence are as sore here as there, and less liberty to look out for a remedy."\*

The discussion was long and anxious. At length the leaders prevail, and a majority vote decides the question. They will go.

But whither? Here was another question difficult of solution. New England never once entered their thoughts; was never

---

\* These are the very words given by Bradford, changed only to the first person and the present tense.

alluded to. Some were for Guiana, "blessed with a perpetual spring," but endangered by the diseases of a tropical climate and exposed to the Spaniard. Others were for some part of Virginia, which was under English rule and already occupied by an English settlement. But here again was a difficulty. The colonizing of Virginia had been under express injunction from the king that all religious services should be held according to the forms of the Church of England. And should persecution arise, it might fare harder with them in that distant land than even in the mother country.

They decide at length for the region held by the Virginia company. But they hope to live in a distinct body by themselves; and they have some friends of "rank and quality" about the court, who "put them in good hope" that they might obtain of his majesty, James, of Hampton Court memory, "free liberty and freedom of religion."

Alas, they did not know that even while they were discussing the proposition, the Solomon of his age was issuing a proclamation (in 1618) requiring the bishop of Lancashire to constrain all the Puritans in that diocese to conform or to leave the country.

What terms they made, the next chapter will reveal.

## CHAPTER VII.

### LONDON.

THE little church had a long negotiation, and a hard bargain at last. For two years the matter was pending, and messengers and communications passing between Leyden and London. They felt, however, that their messengers "also found God going along with them;" and perhaps they had good reason to deem it a special mark of His favor that they were enabled to go at all. The king's disposition towards the Puritans was rather embittered than softened, since he had threatened to harry them out of the land or make them conform. And as the wolf bid the crane be thankful for getting her head safe out of his jaws, so it was a special privilege that James, though he would grant no pledges, was willing to let them alone.

Providentially it was so ordered that the Virginia Company, by reason of their past pecuniary ill success, were extremely anxious to find colonists, and were therefore disposed to do all in their power to favor the enterprise.

Another good providence had seemed to link Scrooby to Plymouth, in giving these friendless men a friend at court. It will be remembered that the last Archbishop of York who occupied the manor-house in which the little church held their first assemblies, was Archbishop Sandys, and that after his death the property passed to his son, Sir Samuel Sandys. Brewster had been for many years a tenant, and unquestionably a trusty tenant, of the latter. In this hour of need, another member of the same family came to their aid. Sir Edwin Sandys, apparently a brother of Sir Samuel, who must have known well the history of this church and probably had personal knowledge of Brewster, a highly religious man as well as a person of ability and influence, was the chief agent in overcoming the difficulties in their way. He was one of the principal members of the Virginia Company. Sandys writes to Robinson and Brewster, after commending the discretion of their agents in 1617, and promising all reasonable aid. "And so I betake you with this design, which I hope verily is the work of God, to the gracious protection and blessing of the highest." They reply, "with all thankful acknowledgment of your singular love, expressing itself, as otherwise, so more specially in your great care and earnest endeavor of our good in this weighty business," and assure him that "under God, above all persons and things in the world we rely upon you, expecting the care of your love, the counsel of your wisdom, and the help and countenance of your authority."

Just before this correspondence, John Carver and Robert Cushman had been sent, at the common expense, to London. Sandys had done his best to secure full religious liberty and "to have it confirmed under the king's broad seal." It was supposed to be practicable. Sandys procured the aid of Sir Robert Naunton, Secretary of State, to intercede with James; and the Archbishop of Canterbury was also approached on the subject. But James was utterly inflexible. They so far prevailed that the king privately agreed to "connive at them and not molest them, provided they carried themselves peaceably." But to tolerate them publicly, under his seal, he would not consent for a moment. Some of their friends hoped that *they* would compromise the difficulty with the Church of England by having their ministers ordained by the bishops; apparently this was a condition made by the archbishop. They could not yield that point. For they held that every pastor is a bishop, and all pastors equal; and that the power to ordain pastors is lodged in the church.

Apparently it required some adroitness in their friends to secure what they did. For when some question was raised in the Privy Council about their religious practices, Robinson and Brewster, in reply, drew up two forms of statement, either to be presented as was thought best, though preferring the shorter and more general one, which was only ten lines in length. But when Sir John Wolstenholme, the gentleman to whom they were sent, had read them both, he declared that he would show neither of them, " lest he should spoil all."

The refusal to pledge toleration was a great disappointment to the church. Some thought their enterprise rested on a pretty "sandy foundation" now. Some regretted that they had ever applied, to be thus refused. But the leaders were resolute. They said that the king was willing enough to leave them unmolested, but was only influenced by reasons of his own for withholding any public declaration. They added, too, that if the king's private assurance, already given, was good for nothing, then "a seal as broad as the house floor" would be equally worthless; for with a disposition to wrong them, there "would be means enough found to recall or reverse it. And they must herein rest on God's providence as they had done in other things."

They determine to rest on God's providence. Cushman and Brewster are dispatched to London to make the business arrangements. But by this time the Virginia company was engaged in an internal broil, and the business was kept in suspense for a year or more. At length when these troubles are settled, a patent is procured from the company, of which the only use was to encourage them for the time; for, being made out in the name of a man who failed of going with him, it became of no value.

But the hardest part was to adjust the penuniary affairs of the expedition. The church had not money enough to emigrate. One Thomas Weston, a London merchant of their acquaintance, whose brother was afterwards a troublesome neighbor at Weymouth in Massachusetts, came to Leyden, and urged them on with large assurances of aid from himself and his business friends. The best thing to be done was to form a joint-stock company in London that should advance the money, while the emigrants should give their personal labor; and in the division of expected profits, each man should draw as much as so many pounds of stock. The arrangement was made accordingly;

but, pressed by their necessities, the colonists were obliged to submit to a very oppressive scheme. Cushman and Carver again were their agents to negotiate this matter; and their efforts are attended with one continued series of annoyances. Indeed Cushman, though an active and an excellent man, proved not to be the most suitable negotiator. Robinson regretted the appointment of Cushman as one of two mistakes which were made, because he was " most unfit to deal for other men by reason of his singularity, and too great indifference for any conditions." A part of this singularity seems to have consisted in the disposition to act on his own single responsibility. For he exceeded his express instructions, and very considerably increased the hardship of the compact.

The Leyden brethren had assented to the sharp bargain whereby *each colonist* should be reckoned in the partnership as equivalent *only to one share of ten pounds*, and in the division of property and profits at the end of seven years should draw only in that proportion. But they insisted that from this division should be exempted their houses, gardens and home fields, to be their own private property; also that two days of each week should be reserved to them from their common-stock labors to expend on their own personal concerns. Cushman, without consulting his clients and therefore contrary to his express instructions, *yielded these two important points*. No doubt he found many difficulties in the way of any arrangement whatever. Some of the largest offers of money had been withdrawn after the long delay, on various pretexts, and concerning a good portion of the promised aid Cushman writes to Carver, " We may go scratch for it." The chief merchant-adventurer, Weston, is lukewarm and does not fulfill his engagements to provide a ship. A general diversity of views and even contention prevails among the members of the joint-stock company in England. So to close the business, and prevent a certain and total failure, as Cushman alleges, he was compelled to waive all conditions.

The church at Leyden, to a man, oppose the concession, and strongly remonstrate with their agent. Nay, some private complaints reached him that he had made "conditions fitter for thieves and bond-slaves than for honest men;" while a series of formal objections is drawn up and sent him. Cushman, whose letters show him to be a little heady, draws up a reply so decidedly tart that, though still preserved, Bradford thinks it never was sent to Leyden, being kept back by Carver. Other letters he did send, and the correspondence between him on the one side, and Bradford, Winslow, Fuller and Allerton, who wrote a joint letter on the other, is not destitute of grim wit.

Cushman demanded their reasons for opposing his settlement, saying they must "think he had no brains;" to which they reply quoting the remark, and " desiring him to exercise his brains therein, referring him to our pastor's former reasons, and then to the censure [judgment] of the godly wise." In a letter which crossed them on the way, (June 10, 1620,) Cushman says he had been so disheartened by discouragements on one side and complaints on the other, that he had declared he would give up his accounts to Carver and quit the whole enterprise, " with only his poor clothes on his back," but he " had gathered up himself by further consideration and resolved to make one trial more;" that on calling upon Mr. Weston, the chief adventurer, he found him so discontented, as to have often said, "but for his promise, he would not meddle with the business further," but he also " at the last gathered up himself a little more, and coming to me two hours after, told me he would not leave it." So they resolved to hire a ship. He and Weston went together and examined a vessel of a hundred and eighty tons, " and a fine ship it is," says Cushman. It was the Mayflower. " And seeing our *near friends there are so strait-laced,* we hope to assure her without troubling them farther; and if the ship prove too small, it fitteth well that such as *stumble at straws already* may rest them there [at Leyden?] awhile, lest worse blocks come in the way ere seven years be ended." Referring again to the complaints, he says: "If men be set on it, let them beat the air; I hope such as are my sincere friends will not think but I can give some reason of my actions. If I do such things as I cannot give reasons for, it is like you have set a fool about your business—and so turn your reproof to yourselves, and send another and let me come again to my combs." (He was a woolcomber.)

In the letter of Bradford and others, just referred to, the community at Leyden expressly "require" Cushman "not to exceed the bounds of your commission, which was to proceed upon the conditions agreed upon and expressed in writing at your going over about it." Unless Mr. Cushman overestimated the trouble, the whole scheme so far as the English adventurers were concerned, was at this time on the verge of dissolution. "To speak the truth, there is fallen already among us a flat schism, and we are readier to go to dispute than to set forward on a voyage." So, believing it, as he affirmed, to be the turning point of the enterprise he did what he was expressly forbidden to do, and yielded the matters in question; "otherwise all had been dashed, and many undone." He meanwhile concealed from his friends at Leyden what he had done, alleging afterwards the want of time to notify them, and the danger of further delay.

The band at Leyden were so opposed to the conditions proposed, that "four or five of the chief" members, even on their arrival in England on the way to Plymouth, "came resolved not to go upon those conditions," the knowledge of which had reached them only through circuitous channels. But, meanwhile, owing to the delay of Weston to provide shipping for the voyage—a matter committed to his charge—and other discouragements experienced, "the state of things at Leyden," Robinson writes to Carver, "is very pitiful; there is great want of money and means to do needful things. Mr. Pickering will not defray a penny here, though Robert Cushman presumed on I know not how many hundred pounds from him and I know not whom." Some who have already paid in part, refuse to advance any more, "till they see shipping provided, or a course taken for it. Nor do I think there is a man here," adds Robinson, "*would pay any thing if he had his money again in his purse.*" This was but six weeks before the time of sailing.

The final settlement of terms in London on the 1st of July, though the nature of the terms was concealed, seems to have set all again in motion. The "fine ship" Mayflower is hired to sail from England, and the little Speedwell, one-third as large, is bought in Holland, to take colonists to join the Mayflower to aid in transporting them, and to remain in America. By the terms arranged in London, there is a seven years' partnership of money and labor, all property for that length of time to be held in common, and at the end of the time to be so divided that the London merchant who invested one hundred pounds, should receive ten times as much as the penniless laborer who gave himself. If, however, the laborer had ten pounds of his own to invest, for that also he should be entitled to a share in the profits. But there was no exemption of their homesteads from the final division, nor of two days in the week for private use, although Mr. Weston had assented to those terms in Leyden, and Mr. Cushman had been expressly required to insist upon them.

It was agreed by the church that but part of them should go now, that part to be the youngest and strongest; that those who went should be volunteers; that the majority should keep the pastor with them, and the minority the elder; that "if [what an IF!] the Lord should frown on our proceedings the colonists should return," and the brethren at Leyden should "assist and be helpful to them; but if God should be pleased to favor them that went, then they also should endeavor to help over such as were poor and ancient and willing to come."

Such were the grave doubts that hung over this bold enterprise from the beginning; and such the difficulties, often completely disheartening, that blocked the way. Yet these are only the beginning of sorrows. What weary, cloudy days—what restless, anxious nights—what plannings and misgivings—what expectations and discouragements—what resolutions and recoils—what fervent prayers to God, hung round that critical step! Is it not always so? Is not every great and good enterprise born among trials and difficulties?

The final determination was not reached till they had held " a solemn meeting and a day of humiliation to seek the Lord for his direction." After a sermon from the beloved Robinson, in which he " strengthened them against their fear and encouraged them in their resolutions," the plans were matured and adopted.

## CHAPTER VIII.

### DELFT HAVEN.

At Delft Haven, fourteen miles south-west of Leyden, lies the Speedwell in the river Meuse. It is the 21st of July. A boat is drawn lazily down the canal to the vessel, laden with the richest freight that ever left the ports of trading Holland. It is the band that now "knew they were PILGRIMS, and lifted up their eyes to the heavens, their dearest country, and quieted their spirits" as they sadly "left that goodly and pleasant city which had been their resting-place near twelve years."

The news had reached Leyden that all was ready. The companions in exile, then to be separated for a time, had " solemnly sought the Lord together." Their pastor took his text from Ezra 8: 21: "And there at the river, by Ahava, I proclaimed a fast, that we might humble ourselves before our God, and seek of him a right way for us, and for our children, and for all our substance." The text, as the reader will find by comparison, was not taken from king James' version—a version made while they were in Holland, though requested in the Conference of Hampton Court—but from the older Geneva version, which " of all translations was the worst," said his majesty, " because of the marginal notes, which allowed disobedience to kings." It was on this occasion that Mr. Robinson gave that memorable address breathing the highest style of Christian magnanimity and marking him as a man in advance of his times.

" Brethren," said Mr. Robinson, " we are now quickly to part from one another, and whether I may ever live to see your faces on earth any more, the God of heaven only knows; but whether the Lord has appointed that or not, I charge you, before God and his blessed angels, that you follow me no farther than you have seen me follow the Lord Jesus Christ.

"If God reveal any thing to you by any other instrument of his, be as ready to receive it as ever you were to receive any truth by my ministry; for I am verily persuaded the Lord has more truth yet to break forth out of his holy Word. For my part I cannot sufficiently bewail the condition of the Reformed Churches who are come to a period in religion, and will go at present no further than the instruments of their reformation. The Lutherans cannot be drawn to go beyond what Luther saw; whatever part of his will our God has revealed to Calvin, they will rather die than embrace it;—and the Calvinists, you see, stick fast where they were left by that great man of God, who yet saw not all things.

"This is a misery much to be lamented; for though they were burning and shining lights, in their times, yet they penetrated not into the whole counsel of God, but were they now living, would be as willing to embrace further light as that which they first received. I beseech you, remember it is an article of your church-covenant, that you receive whatever truth shall be made known to you from the written Word of God. Remember that, and every other article of your sacred covenant. But I must withal exhort you to take heed what you receive as truth; examine it, consider it, and compare it with other scriptures of truth, before you receive it; for it is not possible the Christian world should come so lately out of such anti-christian darkness, and that perfection of knowledge should break forth at once."

And among many other admonitions, not recorded, he urged a hearty co-operation with the non-conforming ministers of the Church of England, whose bishops had driven him and his from their country. "There will be no difference between them and you, when they come to the practice of the ordinances out of the kingdom." And he earnestly advised them "rather to study union with the godly party of the kingdom of England than division," and to see "how near we might possibly without sin close with them, than in the least measure to affect division or separation from them."

On this occasion the pastor's large house was thrown open for a feast given to them by the company that remained. There, says one of the departing band, "we refreshed ourselves, after tears, with singing of psalms, making joyful melody in our hearts as well as with our voices, there being many of our congregation very expert in music; and indeed it was *the sweetest melody that ever mine ears heard.*" Yes, there were many sweet voices there, that never sung together again this side of heaven— many that before a twelvemonth were to sing around the throne of God.

Most of the brethren accompanied or followed them to the harbor of Delft Haven; and some of their friends came thither from Amsterdam, a distance of thirty-six miles, to take leave of them. Again the departing company are "feasted." The long night wears away with "little sleep," but chiefly in "friendly entertainment, Christian discourse, and other real expressions of true Christian love" between those who deeply felt that this might be their last opportunity. Next day the wind is fair. The rising tide warns them on board the Speedwell. Then comes the "sad and mournful parting," with "sighs, and sobs, and prayers," with "tears gushing from every eye," and words "that pierced each heart;" and even the Dutch strangers standing on the wharf and looking on "cannot refrain from tears." The pastor fell "upon his knees—and they all with him—and with watery cheeks commended them with the most fervent prayers to the Lord and his blessing. And then with mutual embraces they took their leave one of another; which proved to be," says Bradford, "the last leave to many of them." Then as the little vessel parted from the wharf, Robinson and his companions stand looking mutely on, "unable to speak one to another for the abundance of sorrow to part." "We gave them," adds Winslow, "a volley of small shot and three pieces of ordnance, and so lifting up our hands to each other and our hearts for each other to the Lord our God, we departed, and found His presence with us in the midst of our manifold straits." A quarter of a century after, as he informs us, the Dutch at Delft

Haven "preserve the memory of the parting." "There was between us that went, and the brethren that stayed, such love as indeed is seldom found on earth." O! sad and mournful parting!

With his accustomed considerateness Mr. Robinson sends by the Speedwell a confidential letter to Mr. Carver, then in England, intended apparently to forestall any apprehension that blame was laid upon him for the change made in the articles of agreement. He says he has a true feeling of Carver's "perplexity of mind and toil of body," recognizes the "great difficulties he had undergone," and congratulates him that he is now to have " the presence and help of so many godly and wise brethren, for bearing your part of the burden, who also will not admit into their hearts the least thought of suspicion of any negligence, at least presumption, to have been in you, whatever they may think in others." He assures him and his "good wife, my loving sister," that "my heart is with you and I will not foreslow [delay] my bodily coming at the first opportunity." "I do ever commend my best affection unto you," continues the loving and beloved pastor to his deacon, "which if I thought you made any doubt of, I would express in more, and the same more ample and full words. And the Lord in whom you trust and whom you serve in this business and journey, guide you with his hand, protect you with his wing, and show you and us his salvation in the end, and bring us in the meanwhile together in the place desired, if such be his good will, for Christ's sake. Amen."

The Mayflower lies at Southampton, three hundred miles distant, on the southern coast of England. A prosperous wind soon brings them thither. Carver, Cushman, Brewster probably, and a few friends direct from England, are waiting for them there. There is "a joyful welcome and mutual congratulations;—and then to "business." How is it about the "alteration of the conditions." Mr. Carver pleaded that he was employed in procuring supplies at Southampton, and had no distinct knowledge of what Mr. Cushman had done at London. Mr. Cushman is in rather an awkward situation; for here are Winslow and Bradford and Fuller and Allerton, the four resolute men that desired him to exercise his brains on their reasons, and required him not to exceed his commission. "We never gave Robert Cushman authority to make one article for us, but only sent him to receive moneys upon articles before agreed upon." How now, Robert Cushman? He says he has "done nothing but what he was urged to partly by the grounds of equity, and more especially by necessity, otherwise all had been dashed and many undone." He also pleads that the other agents were satisfied to leave the management at London in his hands. But why did he not refer the matter to Leyden according to his express instructions? "He could not well in regard to the shortness of the time; and again he knew it would trouble them and hinder the business." They are no better satisfied. Mr. Martin, a new-comer fresh from Billerica in England, rather blunt in his speech, even remarks that "the merchants are blood-suckers" to require such conditions. Mr. Weston also comes up from London to see them off and to have the conditions confirmed. They tell Mr. Weston that "he knew right well that these were not according to the first agreement;" nay, he himself had proposed in Leyden that the colonists should retain their own homesteads—that matter had all been settled before a penny had been advanced. And as they are not at liberty to yield the point without consent of their friends now in Leyden, and indeed had been specially charged by the chief men there, when they came away, not to give their consent, they shall not sign these articles.

Mr. Weston is greatly offended, and tells them they must then "look to stand on their own legs." They still lack a hundred pounds to clear off their debts and leave the port. Weston will not advance a penny for them, but returns to London, leaving them to shift as they could. They sell some sixty or eighty firkins of their butter and raise the money. They also write a manly remonstrance to the merchants, setting forth the facts of the original agreement, but, as matter of conciliation, offering, if the partnership should not prove sufficiently profitable, to continue it after the seven years are expired. As matter of fact the articles are not signed for more than a year. But in November of the following year, moved somewhat perhaps by the persuasions of Mr. Cushman, and magnificent promises from Mr. Weston, (which proved to be but "wind,") and probably still more by the wishes of their friends in Leyden, who may have felt that their own hopes of joining them depended on retaining the good will of the merchants, they signed the hard terms.

When all these business arrangements had been dispatched, oil is poured upon the troubled waters by an affectionate pastoral letter from Mr. Robinson, which was now produced, and in apostolic style read to the whole company.

" Loving Christian friends," it began, " I do heartily and in the Lord salute you all, as being they with whom I am present in my best affection and most earnest longings after you, though I be constrained for awhile to be bodily absent from you. I say constrained, God knowing how willingly, and much rather than otherwise, I would have borne my part with you in this first brunt, were I not by strong necessity held back for the present. Make account of me in the meanwhile, as of a man divided in myself with great pain, and as (natural bonds set aside) having my better part with you."

He exhorts them as the foundation of all other virtue by daily repentance to renew their heavenly peace with God; then by the utmost watchfulness to maintain peace with each other; and not alone by watchfulness against giving offence, but by mutual forbearance against taking offence—a caution the more necessary, he says, both because of the intimate association of so many comparative strangers, and the very nature of their "intended course of civil community." He urges upon them mutual affection to carry on harmoniously their common interests, and the stern repressing of all selfishness; and finally the exercise of great wisdom and godliness in the election of their officers, because "you are to have at least for the present only them for your ordinary governors, whom yourselves shall make choice of for that work."

"These few things," concludes the apostolic man, "I do earnestly commend unto your care and conscience, joining therewith my daily incessant prayer unto the Lord, that He who hath made the heavens and the earth, the sea and all rivers of waters, and whose providence is over all His works, especially over all his dear children for good, would so guide and guard you in your ways, as inwardly by his Spirit, so outwardly by the hand of his power, that both you and we also, for and with you, may have after matter of praising His name all the days of your and our lives. Fare you well in Him in whom you trust, and in whom I rest.

"An unfeigned well-willer of your happy success in this hopeful voyage.

"JOHN ROBINSON."


What a breathing out of Christian wisdom, and of true Christian hopefulness and rest.

## CHAPTER IX.

### THE OCEAN.

The little company sailed out of Southampton harbor, "scarce having any butter, no oil, not a sole to mend a shoe, nor every man a sword by his side, wanting many muskets, much armor"—and depending for future aid on a company of money-making men, already dissatisfied and divided, through whose negligence they shall yet see famine face to face, and, but for the Almighty arm, shall perish. Strong only in God, and their own brave Christian hearts.

It was the fifth of August. In that very month, a Dutch man-of-war was entering James River, Virginia, and landing that ill-fated cargo of TWENTY NEGRO SLAVES, which was the beginning of such long disaster to the western continent. There was the bane, here was the antidote.

Other potent influences are rising or passing away. In England Cromwell has just come of age, and this month he is married. Sir Francis Bacon, an old man of sixty years, has just been condemned for corruption on the bench, and has lain three months in the Tower of London, a disgraced and ruined man. John Milton, a boy of twelve years, is already beginning those midnight studies that impaired his sight with "drop serene;" and Shakspeare has lain four years in his grave. On the Continent the thirty years war is just bursting out, in which all Europe is to be embroiled; while the pusillanimous James, decoyed by the hope of a Spanish bride with two millions dower for his son, looks coldly on and sees his own son-in-law driven a beggar from the throne of Bohemia, and the Protestant cause depressed.

Such was the time when the Pilgrims sailed. Changes have taken place among them since we saw them first. Age is creeping upon Brewster—he is now fifty-six years old; and Mrs. Brewster is in " a weak and decayed state of body." The boy Bradford is now a bold, sagacious man of thirty-two, and by his side stands his wife, Dorothy May. The little John, whom they have so carefully left behind, shall never see his mother again, destined as she is to a watery death on the very coast of the promised land. There is the accomplished and resolute Winslow in the very opening of manhood, also to be a governor and trusty agent of the colony,— and his wife Elizabeth, whose days are numbered. There is the active and enterprising Isaac Allerton, many years the governor's assistant, with Mary his wife and the three young children so soon to be motherless. There is the good soldier Myles Standish, small of stature, but great of heart; and she of whom in less than six months it was written "this day dies Rose, the wife of Captain Standish." There is Samuel Fuller, the beloved physician of the colony, as well as a deacon of the church, who with a prudent forecast has left both wife and child in Leyden. And without enumerating many others less prominent in position or early taken away, there is the good John Carver, a man "of singular piety and rare for humility," laborious and self-sacrificing, who having already spent his estate in the enterprise, will shorten his days in " his care and pains for the common good ;" and as he is among the oldest, so he is among the nearest heaven; and the loving wife, who "being a weak woman," will die " within five or six weeks after him."

Three others at least have left their whole families behind, and several a portion of their children. Among the company are fourteen " servants," and several other persons whose only interest in the enterprise consists in their being hired for certain purposes. There are ten or twelve others pledged apparently by no family ties. And it is sad to see one group of children without father or mother to accompany them—Richard and Jasper and Ellen More and their little brother—divided out in the families of Carver and Brewster and Winslow. Kinder homes they cannot find; yet by another year Richard alone shall be living.

Such, in part, was the company that sailed from Southampton. Their troubles are just begun. The Speedwell speeds ill. Her captain soon complains of a leak, and both vessels put back into the port of Dartmouth. The little vessel is thoroughly examined and repaired. Eight precious days, with a fair wind, are lost. Perhaps no better picture can be given of the discouragements they encountered from without and from the influence of at least one leading man within, than is presented in a letter written from this port of Dartmouth by the officious and peremptory but now faint-hearted Robert Cushman. The reader, in perusing its statements, will make some allowance for the "bundle of lead crushing his heart," and do him the justice to remember that after these few trying weeks were over, he continued to be, says Bradford, "a special instrument for their good, and to do the offices of a loving friend and brother."

"Loving friend"—writes Mr. Cushman to Edward Southworth—"my most kind remembrance to you and your wife, with loving E. M., etc., whom in this world I never look to see again. For besides the imminent dangers of this voyage, which are no less than deadly, an infirmity of body hath seized me which will not in all likelihood leave me till death. What to call it I know not, but it is a bundle of lead, as it were, crushing my heart more and more these fourteen days, [ever since the talk about " the conditions,"] so that although I do the actions of a living man, yet I am but as dead;—but the will of God be done. Our pinnace will not cease leaking, else I think we had been half way to Virginia; our voyage hither hath been as full of crosses as ourselves have been of crookedness. We put in here to trim her, and I think, as others also, that if we had staid but three or four hours more, she would have sunk right down. And though she was twice trimmed at Hampton, yet now she is open and leaky as a sieve; and there was a board a man might have pulled off with his fingers, two foot long, where the water came in as at a mole-hole. We lay at Hampton seven days in fair weather, waiting for her; and now we lie here waiting for her in as fair a wind as can blow, and so have done these four days and are likely to lie four more, and by that time the wind will haply turn as it did at Hampton.

"Our victuals will be half eaten up, I think, before we go from the coast of England, and if our voyage last long, we shall not have a month's victuals when we come into the country. Near seven hundred pound hath been bestowed at Hampton, upon what I know not. Mr. Martin saith he neither can nor will give any account of it. [Martin had never been with the Pilgrims in Holland, but for prudential reasons, as he and some of his friends were going in the company, had been designated with Carver and Cushman to lay in provisions. He would seem to have been a little self-sufficient, and perhaps Cushman's complaints of him are not without some reason. But Mr. Cushman shall tell his own story. He proceeds.] And if he be called on for accounts he crieth out of unthankfulness for his pains and care, that we are suspicious of him—and flings away, and will end nothing. And so he insulteth over our poor people with such scorn and contempt, as if they were not good enough to wipe his shoes. It would break your heart to see his dealing, and the mourning of our people. They complain to me, and alas I can do nothing for them. If I speak to him, he flies in my face as mutinous, and saith no complaints shall be heard but by himself, and they are froward and discontented and waspish and discontented people, and I do ill to hear them. [Mr. Martin probably was the "governor" in the Speedwell.] There are others that would lose all they have put in, or make satisfaction for what they have had, that they might depart, [the writer probably was one;] but he will not hear them nor suffer them to go ashore lest they should run away. The sailors also are offended at his ignorant boldness, in meddling and controlling things he knows not what belongs to, so that some threaten to mischief him; others say they will leave the ship and go their way. But at the best this cometh of it, that he makes himself a scorn and laughing-stock unto them. As for Mr. Weston, except grace do greatly sway with him, he will hate us ten times more than ever he loved us, for not confirming the conditions."

Mr. Cushman even speaks with some dissatisfaction of Mr. Robinson as being "in the fault, who charged them never to consent to the conditions, nor choose me into office [on shipboard,] but appointed them to choose those they did choose;"—on which statement Bradford remarks, "I think he (Cushman) was deceived in these things." Cushman—after predicting that "he (Robinson) and they will rue too late that they were so ignorant, yea, so inordinate in their courses"—returns to his complaints of Mr. Martin for having expended "money so rashly and lavishly, without knowing how he comes by it or on what conditions;" and proceeds:

"I told him of the alteration [of the articles] long ago, and he was content. But now he domineers and said I had betrayed them into the hands of slaves—he is not beholden to them [the merchants]—he can set out two ships himself to a voyage. When, good man? He hath but twenty pound in, and if he should give up his accounts, he would not have a penny left him, as I am pursuaded. ['This was found true afterward,' writes Bradford.]

"*Friend, if ever we make a plantation, God works a miracle;* especially considering how scant we shall be of victuals and most of all ununited among ourselves, and devoid of good tutors and regiment [governors and government.] Violence will break all. Where is the meek and humble spirit of Moses? and of Nehemiah, who re-edified the walls of Jerusalem, and the state of Israel?

Is not the sound of Rehoboam's brags daily here among us? Have not the philosophers and all wise men observed that even in settled commonwealths, violent governors bring either themselves or their people or both to ruin? How much more in the raising of commonwealths, when the mortar is scarce yet tempered that should bind the walls?

"If I should write to you of all things which *promiscuously forerun our ruin*, I should overcharge my weak head and your tender heart; only this, prepare for evil tidings of us every day. But pray for us instantly; it may be the Lord will be entreated one way *or the other* for us. I see not in reason how we shall escape even the gasping of hunger-starved persons; but God can do much, and his will be done. It is better for me to die, than now for me to bear it, which I do daily and expect it hourly; having received sentence of death, both within and without me. Poor William King and myself do strive *who shall be meat first for the fishes;* but we look for a glorious resurrection, knowing Christ Jesus after the flesh no more, but looking unto the joy that is set before us, we will endure all these things and account them light in comparison of that joy we hope for. Remember me in all love to our friends as if I named them, whose prayers I desire earnestly and wish again to see, but not till I can with more comfort look them in the face. The Lord give us that true comfort which none can take from us.

"I had a desire to make a brief relation of our estate to some friend. I doubt not but your wisdom will teach you seasonably to utter things as hereafter you shall be called to it. That which I have written is true, and many things more which I have forborne. I write it as upon my life, and last confession in England. What is of

use to be spoken of presently, *you may speak of it;* and what is fit to conceal, conceal. Pass by my weak manner; for my head is weak, and my body feeble. The Lord make me strong in him, and keep both you and yours. Your loving friend,
"Robert Cushman.
"*Dartmouth,* August 17, 1620."

Making all allowance for the coloring of this letter, it certainly gives a glimpse of a truly dismal prospect. Losing precious time, short of supplies, with a leaky ship, leading merchants disaffected, unsympathizing governor and a grumbling crew in the Speedwell, a busy and talkative agent ready to hear if not to foment complaints, and prophesying certain and dismal ruin. Probably it was well for the little band to undergo, as it did, a further sifting. Brave hearts and strong were needed for their work.

Robert Cushman was not destined to become "meat for fishes;" he was not destined to "the gasping of hunger-starved persons," nor to be overwhelmed by the "bundle of lead, as it were, crushing his heart." He was preserved to do good service yet, and to be "the right arm" of the colony with the merchant adventurers, and, some five or six years later to lay his bones in the mother country, as he was about finally to join his brethren. Deliverance to him was nearer probably than he thought— although there are obscure hints in the close of his letter that look towards a return.

Again they launch. A hundred leagues are made, when again the Speedwell leaks so badly that the captain declares he must bear up or sink at sea. They put back to Plymouth, and examine the ship again. No special leak is found; and indeed when the Speedwell was sold, she made many profitable voyages. But they determine at length to abandon the vessel on the ground of "general weakness." Well they may. For though abundantly capable of "many voyages," she was incapable of that one. It was pre-arranged that she should leak. The captain and crew understood the trick of having her "over-masted and too much pressed with sails," till the strain brought the water pouring in through her seams. They were intimidated at the fear of want, as the vessel was to remain, and the crew to stay with her for a year. So they had "plotted this stratagem."

It became necessary with the smaller vessel to dismiss a portion of the passengers. Twenty persons are left, most of them "willing" to go back from "discontent or fear;" but there were some dismissed, who, on account of "their own weakness and charge of many young children, were thought least useful and most unfit to bear the brunt of this hard adventure—unto which work of God, and judgment of their brethren they were contented to submit." Among the number willing to remain were Mr. Cushman and his family. There was another "sad parting," ominous of ill. The hospitality of friends in Plymouth, by whom they "were kindly entertained and courteously used," was afterwards commemorated in the name of their own American home.

The stormy month of September arrived before they left the harbor. Besides the crew, one hundred and two persons, with all their effects and supplies, are crowded into that little vessel; and a birth and a death on board keep their number good to the end. Before long, "cross winds and many fierce storms" overtake them. The upper works of the ship grow leaky, and by the severe shaking "one of the main beams in the midships is bowed and cracked." The muttering sailors express their fears; and "a serious consultation" is held with the officers of the ship, attended with "great difference of opinion among the mariners themselves." The officers aver that the ship is "strong and firm under water;" and the carpenter promises that with a great iron screw belonging to the passengers he will bring the beam to its place. The upper works can be caulked, and though with the working of the ship they will not long keep staunch, yet there would be no great danger if they did not over-press her with sails. So they committed themselves to the will of God, and resolved to proceed"—for they were now in mid-ocean. Often for days together "the winds were so fierce and the seas so high that they could not bear a knot of sail."

The tedium of the voyage is diversified, if not relieved, by the sallies of one profane and brutal sailor, who, during their seasickness, daily loaded them "with grievous execrations," expressing his hope " to cast

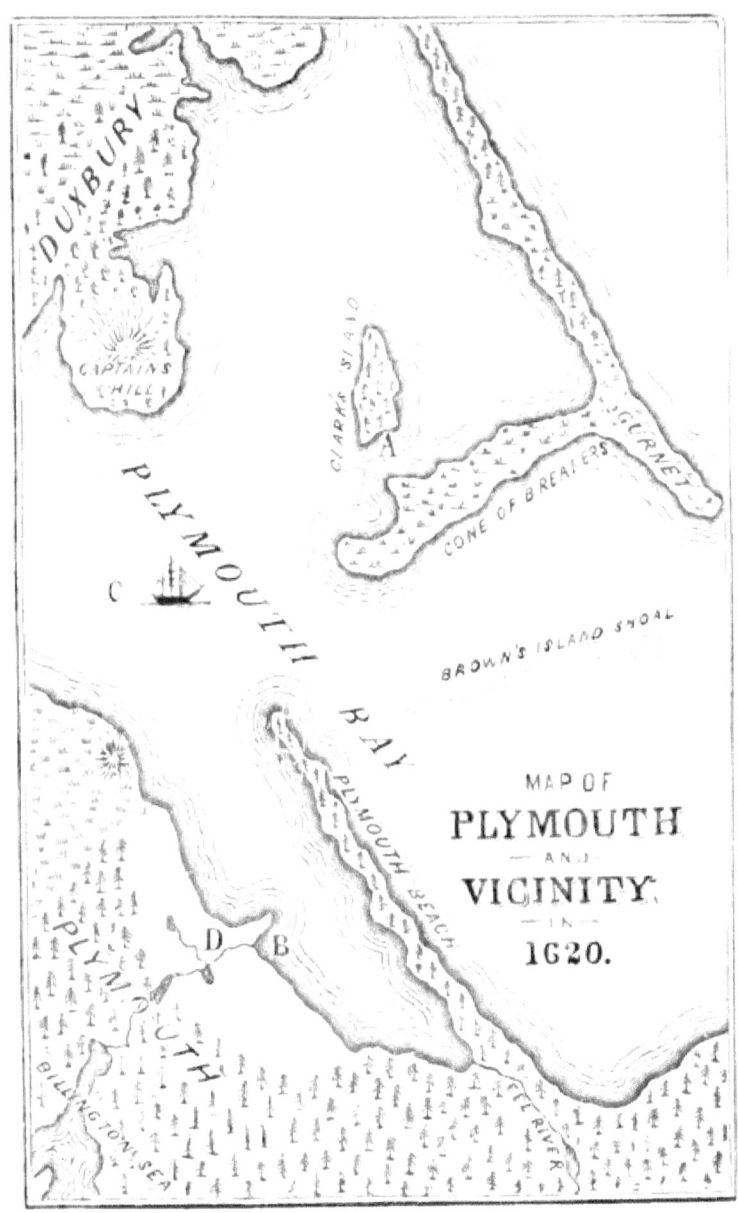

Pilgrim Church.    pp. 181.

half of them overboard before they came to their journey's end," and, if gently reproved, cursing and swearing. bitterly. "But it pleased God before they came half seas over to smite this young man with a grievous disease of which he died in a desperate manner, and so was himself the first that was thrown overboard," and his fellows noted it to be the just hand of God upon him." The seamen appear, on other occasions, to have caught the spirit of the merchant-adventurers, and to have shown them little kindness.

Sixty-four long days are passed, when, on the 9th of November they were made "not a little joyful" by the sight of land. It was Cape Cod. They are bound for the mouth of the Hudson. After a dangerous entanglement, as they thought it, in shoals and breakers, they were constrained to return, and were next day safely moored in Cape Cod Harbor. And before all other proceedings, "they fell down on their knees and blessed the Lord, the God of Heaven, who had brought them over the vast and furious ocean, and delivered them from all perils and miseries thereof."

## CHAPTER X.

### THE LAND.

They knew that they had abundant cause of gratitude; and so they gave thanks to God. But there was a vast deal more to be thankful for than they then knew—or ever knew.

It ought never to be forgotten that the first settlement of New England was in its chief aspect a missionary enterprise. Even the subordinate reasons rendered, resolve themselves into a desire of these men to make the most of themselves and theirs for the cause of God; while, before leaving Holland, they had themselves thus expressed their chief inducement: "Lastly, (and which was not the least,) a great hope and inward zeal they had of laying some good foundation, or at least to make some way thereunto for *propagating and advancing the gospel of the kingdom of Christ* in those remote parts of the world; yea, though they should be but even as stepping-stones unto others for the performing of so great a work." This motive is too repeatedly and prominently set forth to be for one moment mistaken.

They never knew how wonderfully God was about to answer their prayer, nor unto what great religious results he was making them the "stepping-stones." Consequently they never saw the bearing of some of the chief dealings of God's providence on the very end they had in view. God had carefully kept the land for the men. How he had locked up the whole continent from the knowledge of Europe till fifty years after the discovery of printing, and on the eve of the great Reformation. And how carefully then he had shut it up from all attempts at permanent colonization till the ripest fruits of the Reformation had been gathered. For more than a hundred years after its discovery, no European was suffered to get a foothold in North America. There were attempts enough. For two-thirds of a century the monarchy of France and the chivalry of Spain had vainly sought to establish permanent colonies in the country. God kept the land for the hour and the men.

The men—the first permanent colonists of North America—had already been chosen from that nation of all Europe, in which on the whole the rights of man had made the highest progress, and the claims of God were best understood.

And now the fathers of New England had been taken from the best, the Puritan, party of that nation; and even of that party, these were the men most thoroughly sifted and tried and trained. They were sent from England when the British mind was in the very bloom and flush of strength—when

Shakspeare, Bacon, Raleigh, Hampden, Cromwell, all were living. They were sent by Holland to chasten their spirits and broaden their views. They were sent through opposition, hardship, and poverty, to keep them from being overrun by worthless adventurers, and were long hedged round by a wall of suffering to work out their grand experiment unmolested. A promiscuous rush of colonists in their train might have changed the destinies of New England—and of how much else? Indeed, the Omniscient Eye carefully watched the whole course of events; in a quarter of a century God suffered but about 21,000 men to follow them—men chiefly of kindred mind—and then by his wise providence he shut off the stream of emigration.

God had led them not only by a way, but to a place they knew not. They were looking much further south—at least to the mouth of the Hudson. They were brought to a better place for them—where there should be none to dispute possession, and where they and theirs might long remain undisturbed, a peculiar people. Perhaps they had reason to be thankful that God brought them to one of the barrenest portions of the continent. How much the virtue of their descendants has clung to that barren soil—or how the whole future of the great Puritan family would have been changed had the forefathers fallen upon some luxuriant Guiana or Florida—who but God can tell.

And as God led them to that spot, how carefully had he cleared the place—though they knew it not. He had left the savages to subdue the wild beasts of the forest, till about three years before, and then by a terrible pestilence that almost annihilated some of the tribes, he had nearly cleared that whole coast of the enemies that not only might, but doubtless would have devoured them in their feeble state. There were times when even the feeble remnant could have crushed them as they would an infant. In the spot soon fixed upon for the colony, the plague had left " not one man, woman or child remaining." All the delays and difficulties of the embarkation, and cross-winds of the voyage, had been needful to bring them to this place. Had they made an earlier arrival, they would have gone to the southward. Necessity brought them here.

Notwithstanding they knew not or considered not all these things, these men felt that they had abundant reason for gratitude. And they gave hearty thanks; for no men ever more thoroughly acknowledged the daily providential hand of God.

And yet if they rejoiced in God, it was not without the deepest sense of their forlorn condition. Here is the picture drawn long afterwards by one of those very men: " Here I cannot but stay and make a pause and stand half amazed at these poor people's condition. For having passed through many troubles both before and upon the voyage, as aforesaid, they had now no friends to welcome them, nor inns to entertain and refresh them, no houses, much less towns to repair unto to seek for succor. It is recorded in Scripture as a mercy to the apostle and his ship-wrecked company that 'the barbarians showed them no small kindness' in refreshing them. But these savage barbarians, when they met with them, were readier to fill their sides full of arrows, than otherwise. And for the season, it was winter; and they that know the winters of that country, know them to be sharp and violent and subject to violent storms, dangerous to travel to known places, much more to search out unknown coasts. Besides, what could they see, but a hideous and desolate wilderness full of wild beasts and wild men? and what multitudes there might be of them they knew not. Neither could they, as it were, go up to the top of Pisgah, to view from this wilderness a more goodly country to feed their hopes. For which way soever they turned their eyes, *save upward to the heavens*, they could have little solace or content in respect to any outward objects. For, summer being done, all things stand for them to view with a weather-beaten face ; and the whole country being full of woods and thickets, presented a wild and savage hue. If they looked behind them there was the mighty ocean which they had passed, and was now a main bar and gulf to separate them from all the civil [civilized] parts of the world. If it be said they had a ship to succor them—it is true ; but what heard they daily from the master and company but that with speed they should look out a place for their shallop, where they would be at some near distance ; for the season was such that he would not stir from thence until a safe harbor was discovered by them, where they would be, and he might go without danger; and that victuals consumed apace, but *he must and would keep sufficient for himself and company* for their return. Yea, it was muttered by some, that if they got not a place in time, they [the ship's crew] would turn them and their goods on shore *and leave them.* Let it also be considered what weak hopes of supply and succor they left behind them, that might bear up their minds in this sad condition, and the trials they were under. It is true, indeed, the affection and love of their brethren at Leyden were cordial and entire; but they had little power to help them, or themselves; and how the case stood between them and the merchants at their coming away, hath already been declared. What could now sustain them but the Spirit of God and his grace?"

It would seem as though little could be added to the desolateness of the picture: a feeble company, scantily supplied with provisions, on a wilderness shore, in the opening of winter; none but hostile savages to receive them; a threatening crew pressing them to land; not a shelter ready nor even a site selected for their home; the captain refusing to move his vessel from her moorings, and their exploring " shallop " requiring a fortnight's precious time to repair; with not a sympathetic heart except the band almost as helpless as themselves, across the water—lying at the mercy of an unsympathizing, disaffected corporation. But still one other thing is added: faction in their own little number. Few as they were, there was discordant material among them. There were "strangers" who had joined them in England, some of them employed for hire, and one or two surreptitiously crowded in by friends in England. These men had dropped "discontented and mutinous speeches," declaring that as the patent was for Virginia and not for New England, and consequently they were beyond its reach, "none had power to command them," and "when they came on shore they would use their own liberty."

Troubles were thick. But these were not the men to lie still in despair. They took each thing in its order. First the faction was silenced. For this purpose, before any foot pressed the shore, that famous "compact" was drawn, which, avowing that they have undertaken to plant a colony "for the glory of God and the advancement of the Christian faith, and the honor of our king and country," binds them together as "a civil body politic" to enact "just and equal laws" "for the general good," to which they "promise all due submission and obedience." This document, equally remarkable for its declaration of their religious purpose, and its utterance, in the fewest words, of the very essence of a republican government, was signed by forty-one names—the adult male members of the company. John Carver is chosen Governor.

Now for work. The shallop is hauled out for an exploring trip; unfortunately she needs sixteen days' work in repairing. No time is to be lost. A band of sixteen men, with Standish at their head, set forth by land. The women hasten ashore to do their washing. But, alas, at every passage from the ship to the land in that shallow water, there is a long way to wade, and many a death-cold is thus early taken.

We do not propose to follow all the incidents of their daily toils.

The most noticeable things which the exploring party saw were the numerous graves that marked, although they knew it not, the late terrible mortality. The first welcome to their new land was a shower of arrows that came rattling around their camp-fire one morning at day-break. At five o'clock that morning they had already held their morning prayers, in haste for an early departure; but they pause after the attack to "give God solemn thanks and praise for their deliverance," not a man being hit or hurt, though several of their coats that hung on the wall of the enclosure were "shot through and through." The savages had aimed at some of the chief men of the colony. The special providence of God, as they felt it to be, directed them to a large quantity of buried Indian corn. They took it, with the settled purpose of making "large satisfaction" to the owner, whenever he could be found; and it was their sole supply of seed-corn for the year ensuing. But for this, says Bradford, "they might have starved." The Lord, he adds, "is never wanting unto his in their greatest needs; let his holy name have all the praise." They afterwards paid the Indians what the savages deemed double the value of the corn.

From the time of the encounter with the Indians they proceed only in the shallop. Fifteen leagues they coast along, but find no harbor. A storm of sleet and rain comes on—the wind is high and the sea is rough. With a broken rudder they press all sail to gain an expected shelter, when the mast breaks, the sail goes overboard, and they narrowly, "by God's mercy," escape being cast away—Carver, and Bradford, and Winslow and Standish among them. Again they barely miss being wrecked in the breakers; and in deep darkness and a pitiless rain they run under a lee shore. Fear of the Indians warned them to spend the night upon the boat. But human nature could hold out no longer. Many of them were so weak and cold that they hurried on shore and with much difficulty lighted a fire; and the whole company followed. "God gave them a morning of comfort and refreshing." The sun shone out clear and frosty. They found themselves secure upon an island—Clark's Island—at the entrance of the beautiful harbor of Plymouth. The day is devoted to resting their weary frames, drying their effects, putting their arms in order, and giving "God thanks for his mercies in their manifold deliverances." The following day was the Sabbath. But though they were all rested, and their errand most pressing, and their friends anxiously waiting for their return, not a foot moved on its way. *They kept holy the day of the Lord.* Upon the strict piety that thus loved the duties of the sacred Sabbath and reverenced God and his ordinances, depended the character of New England.

On Monday the 11th of December, (the memorable 22d, new style, as it is now reckoned—though it should be the 21st,) they landed on Plymouth Rock. They sounded the harbor and marched into the land, till they were satisfied they had found the place for their home; then hurried back to "comfort the hearts" of their friends. There was one heart among themselves that needed comfort: the loving wife who should have welcomed William Bradford back, met him no more—she had been drowned in his absence.

In a few days more, (on Saturday the 16th,) the Mayflower rides at anchor in the new-found harbor. Again the holy Sabbath intervenes, and fills their hearts with peace and courage and strength for the morrow. Monday and Tuesday are spent in exploring the region to fix on a village site. There is no time to lose in search or deliberation, "our victuals being much spent." Two places are in question. So on Wednesday morning " after we had called on God for direction," we " go ashore again " and fix upon a site " on a high ground, where there is a great deal of land cleared, and that hath been planted with corn three or four years ago; and there is a very sweet brook runs under the hill side, and many delicate springs of as good water as can be drunk, and where we may harbor our shallops and boats exceeding well; and in this brook much good fish in their seasons; on the further side of the river also much corn-ground cleared. In one field is a great hill on which we point [appoint] to make a platform and plant our ordnance [cannon] which will command all about. From thence we may see into the bay, and far into the sea; and we may see thence Cape Cod. Our greatest labor will be the fetching of our wood, which is half a quarter of an English mile. What people inhabit here we know not, for as yet we have seen none. So there we made our rendezvous, resolving in the morning to come all ashore and build houses."

That was Plymouth.

## CHAPTER XI.

### HOME.

But the next day it rained and blew tempestuously — and the next also. In the midst of the storm the birth of a dead son to Isaac Allerton sadly inaugurates the founding of a new home.

When the storm clears off, all hands are on shore, "some to fell timber, some to saw, some to rive, and some to carry; so no man rested that day." Many of them, too, were men who had seldom done such work. Amid the "frost and foul weather" of midwinter, so hindering them that they could "seldom work half the week," Leyden Street is lined with its "common-house" twenty feet square, and its little row of dwellings packed snugly by each other's side for mutual security. Nineteen dwellings seem to have been in their plan, but when the Spring came they had built, and they required, not half the number. In less than one month from the day when the first tree fell, they hold their Sabbath worship on the shore. The work goes on under great difficulties. John Goodman wanders away and freezes his feet. William Bradford, by reason of his late exposures, is " vehemently seized with grief and pain" which " so shot to his huckle-bone, [hip-bone,] it was doubted he would have died instantly." The thatched roof takes fire when Carver and Bradford lie sick among loaded muskets, and their lives are endangered; but " through God's mercy they had no harm." A furious storm washes out the clay mortar with which the crevices of their log-houses are filled. Again the thatch of their sick-house takes fire, but no harm is done.

Pilgrim Church   pp. 203.

And all the while, there are glimpses and sounds of savages flitting ghostlike round them in the distance, and filling them with apprehensions; till at length one "fair warm day" in March, Samoset marches boldly through the village to the very rendezvous where the men are perfecting their military organization, and loudly bids them "welcome." It is the beginning of a firm and lasting peace with the neighboring Indians; and Squanto, sole known survivor of those who once tilled the corn-lands of Plymouth, teaches them how to plant their fields.

But long before the young blade is up, the Reaper whose name is death, had thrust in his sickle; and before the month of November came round, fifty-one of the one-hundred-and-two lay beneath the turf. Hardship and exposure did their work, indeed, chiefly before the end of March. The whole family of Mr. Martin became extinct. Priscilla Molines is the only survivor of her father's house. John Turner and his two sons, Thomas Tinker with his wife and only child, John and Edward Tillie and their wives, John Rigdale and wife, James Chilton and wife, Edward Fuller and wife, the noble John Carver and his wife, and three of the four orphan children were cut down. Mrs. White was written a widow; and the wives of Standish, Bradford, Winslow, Allerton, and Francis Eaton had finished their brief course. In the time of greatest distress, Brewster and Standish and five other individuals alone were well enough to wait upon the rest. "The Lord upheld these persons" while they "spared no pains night or day, but with abundance of toil and hazard of their own health, fetched them wood, made them fires, dressed them meat, made their beds, washed their loathsome clothes, clothed and unclothed them, in a word did all homely and necessary offices for them, and all this willingly and cheerfully, without any grudging in the least, showing herein their true love unto their friends and brethren."

Meanwhile a very different scene was taking place on ship-board. When the sickness began on the land, one of the sufferers—Bradford himself—had desired "a small can of beer" from the supply on board, but had received answer from "the master" that "if he were his own father he should have none." But before the vessel was ready to sail the disease broke out among the crew. And now for the spirit of selfishness. These "boon companions in drinking and jollity" dreading infection, "began now to desert one another in this calamity, saying they would not hazard their lives for them by coming to help them in their cabins, but if they died, let them die." But the passengers showed them the kindness and attention which they could not gain from their own friends, and melted some of their selfish hearts. Among others, the boatswain, who had often scoffed and cursed at the passengers, confessed that "he did not deserve this at their hands—he had abused them in word and deed." "O!" exclaimed he, "you show your love like Christians indeed to one another, but we let one another lie and die like dogs." The poor fellow died, and with him about half the crew. The dead were buried on the bank that overhangs the landing.

It is a sad picture of the weakness of the colony, that, fearing lest the Indians should learn their prostrate condition, the graves on the bank were levelled that spring, and the ground above was sown with grain. Human bones have been repeatedly washed from the bank; and in the summer of 1855, when a drain was dug through the spot, the remains of several human beings were found and deposited, as sacred dust, on "Burial

Hill." "The spring advancing, it pleases God the mortality begins to cease, and the sick and lame recover." It "puts new life into the people." On the fifth of April the Mayflower left the harbor on her homeward voyage; but though many a watery eye must have watched her till she was lost to the sight, not one of the survivors abandoned the place now hallowed by suffering. "It was the Lord which upheld them," writes one who was himself brought low with sickness, "and had beforehand prepared them; many having long borne the yoke, yea, from their youth." It was a special mercy to the little colony that, with the exception of Mr. Carver, all the leading men were spared. Had even five or six of the more responsible members been cut off, what might have been the issue, none but He who ordered all, can tell.

As the autumn came on, it found them in plenty; with a good crop, a successful beaver-trade, abundance of fish, and a supply of water fowls and wild turkeys. "And thus," say they, "they found the Lord to be with them in all their ways, and to bless their outgoings and their incomings, for which let his holy name have the praise forever, to all posterity."

So, "our harvest being gotten in, [twenty acres of Indian corn, and six acres of barley and peas,] our governor sent four men on fowling, that so we might after a special manner rejoice together after we had gathered the fruit of our labors. They four in one day killed as many fowl as, with a little help beside, served the company almost a week. At which time, among other recreations, we exercised our arms, many of the Indians coming among us, and among the rest their greatest king, Massasoit, with some ninety men, whom for three days we entertained and feasted; and they went out and killed five deer, which they brought to the plantation, and bestowed on our governor, and upon the captain and others. And although it be not always so plentiful as it was at this time with us, yet by the goodness of God, we are so far from want, that we often wish you, [our distant friends,] partakers of our plenty."

Thus wrote Winslow to his friend Morton in December, 1621. But his exultant words were a little premature. The plenty was diminishing before the letter was sent. The ship Fortune, by which it was dispatched, had brought thirty-six more colonists and no supplies—"not so much as a biscuit-cake or any other victuals for them; neither had they any bedding but some sorry things they had in their cabins, nor pot, nor pan, nor any thing to dress their meat in; nor over-many clothes, for many of them had brushed away their coats and cloaks at Plymouth as they came." However, they were mostly able-bodied young men; and "the plantation was glad of this addition to their strength." An almost double number of consumers makes a speedy difference in the provisions; and the Governor is obliged to put all on half allowance with the prospect at that rate of only six months' supply.

The Fortune also brought a harsh letter from Mr. Weston, complaining of the transactions before they sailed, and chiding them because, in the labors and sickness of the winter, they had been unable to lade the Mayflower with a valuable freight. He had learned, of course, from the crew of the ship the prostrate condition of the colony, yet he sees fit to address Governor Carver in the following style: "That you sent no lading in the ship is wonderful and worthily distasted. I know your weakness was the cause of it, and I believe more weakness of judgment than weakness of hands. A quarter of the time you spent in discoursing, arguing and consulting, would have done much more."

And he goes on to assure them that if they will sign "the conditions" and send a good lading in this ship, to requite his expenditures and encourage the company, he "*will never quit the business though all the other adventurers should.*"

They freighted back the Fortune "with good clapboard as full as she could stow, and two hogshead of beaver and otter skins;" the whole lading being valued at five hundred pounds. But as to Mr. Weston's valiant assurances, "all proved but wind," says Bradford, "for he was the first and only man that forsook them, and that before he so much as heard of the return of the ship or knew what was done; so vain is the confidence in man."

To Mr. Weston's complaints, Governor Bradford writes in a manly and touching strain—with a single burst of honest indignation. The last sentence of the extract is one of the indications that even into their little number there had crept individuals with whom they had nothing in common. The Billington family, for example, had "been shuffled into their company" by friends in London. The father was a profane and troublesome "knave," who, after causing continual annoyance to the colony, ten years later was hung for murder. But to the letter of Bradford to Weston:—

"Sir: Your large letter written to Mr. Carver I have received, wherein (after the apology made for yourself) you lay many heavy imputations upon him and upon us all. Touching him, he is departed this life, and is now at rest in the Lord from all those troubles and incumbrances with which we are yet to strive. He needs not my apology; for his care and pains were so great for the common good, both ours and yours, that therewith, it is thought, he oppressed himself and shortened his days; of whose loss we cannot sufficiently complain [deplore]. At great charges in this adventure, I confess you have been, and many losses may sustain; but the loss of his and many other honest and industrious men's lives cannot be valued at any price. Of the one there may be hope of recovery, but the other no recompense can make good. But I will not insist on generals, but will come now to particulars.

"You greatly blame us for keeping the ship so long in the country, and then to send her away empty. She lay five weeks at Cape Cod, while with many a weary step and the endurance of many a hard brunt, we sought out in the foul winter a place of habitation. Then we went in so tedious a time to make provision to shelter us and our goods, about which labor many of our arms and legs can tell us to this day we were not negligent. But it pleased God to visit us then with death daily, and with so general a disease that the living were scarce able to bury the dead, and the well not in any measure sufficient to tend the sick. And now to be so greatly blamed for not freighting the ship, doth indeed go near us and much discourage us. But you say you know we will pretend weakness; and do you think we had not cause? Yes, you tell us you believe it, but it was more weakness of judgment than of hands. Our weakness herein is great, we confess, therefore we will bear this check patiently till God send us wiser men. But they which told you we spent so much time in discoursing and consulting, &c., their hearts can tell their tongues, they lie. They cared not, so they might salve their own sores, how they wounded others. Indeed, it is our calamity that we are (beyond expectation) yoked with some ill-conditioned people who will never do good, but corrupt and abuse others."

In the same letter the Governor informs him that they have at length signed the articles; exhibits the condition of affairs, and apprises him distinctly that unless they had supplies in due time the addition to their numbers must "unavoidably bring famine upon them."

Hardly had the vessel sailed and the company been put on short allowance, when the Narraganset tribe of Indians, covering the whole State of Rhode Island and numbering thirty thousand, offended at their friendly relations to certain other tribes, sent them a messenger with a bundle of arrows tied with a snake-skin. The Governor of this little band of eighty-seven men, women and children, by advice of others, "sent a round answer" to the tribe that mustered five thousand warriors, "that if they rather have war than peace they might begin when they would; they had done them no wrong, neither did they fear them." He also sent back the skin of the rattle-snake, stuffed with powder and balls. But the colony at once surround their dwellings with a strong stockade, with gates that were shut and guarded every night; and their military organization was arranged anew by Captain Standish. The Narragansets, however, had a mysterious horror of powder and ball. So when the snake-skin came back, Canonicus the chief would not touch it nor leave it in his wigwam, but ordered the messenger to take it home. On his refusal, it was passed from hand to hand till it reached the settlement again. The sight of gunpowder did the business, and the Narragansets kept their distance.

In these anxieties in their relations to the savages and the merchants, the Governor was not without his grave joke. On Christmas day he summoned the people to their toil as usual—for Christmas day they held in no esteem. But most of the new-comers, who seem to have been direct from England, "excused themselves, and said it went against their consciences to work on that day. So the Governor told them that if they made it matter of conscience he would spare them till they were better informed. And he led away the rest and left them. But when they came home from their work at noon he found them in the street at play openly, some pitching the bar, some at stoolball, and such like sports. So he went to them, and took away their implements, and told them that was against his conscience that they should play and others work. If they made the keeping of it matter of devotion, let them keep their houses, but there should be no gaming or revelling in the streets."

The second season wore away. The supplies for which they looked did not come. Instead of aid came a fishing vessel of Mr. Weston, sent out on his own account, and letters from him, first advising them to break their compact with the merchants, afterwards informing them that he had quit the company. Letters from Cushman and three other individuals inform them, moreover, that Mr. Weston is about sending a colony of his into their neighborhood, under the charge of Weston's brother, "a heady young man and violent, and set against you there," and that the most of his colony are "not fit for an honest man's company." Mr. Weston himself admits in one of his letters that they are "rude fellows," but he hopes " not only to be able to reclaim them from that profaneness that may scandalize the voyage, but by degrees to draw them to God, &c." He asks the Plymouth men to give them entertainment.

They were greatly at a loss what to do—advised as they were by their friends in England in the strongest terms to have nothing to do with this rude company, both for their own sakes and anticipated trouble with the Indians which such a set of men must produce. But they concluded to give them friendly entertainment, partly in consideration of their earlier relations to Mr. Weston, and partly in compassion to the strangers themselves, thrown otherwise friendless on the coast, though with abundant supplies. So they endured them through the summer—though the newcomers meanly stole the green corn and impaired the harvest;—and they took care of their sick for some time after the departure of the new colony to Weymouth. These "rude fellows"—to follow their history a little—in a few months squandered their abundant supplies, and came to utter destitution. They sold even their clothing and bedding to the Indians, became their servants, cutting wood and bringing water "for a cap full of corn," and at length resorted to stealing. Notwithstanding every device, many of them perished with cold and hunger. As they wandered on the shore hunting for clams and ground nuts, one of them was so weak that he stuck fast in the mud, and was found lying dead. They embroiled themselves with the Indians, according to the predictions of all who knew them ; and a plot was formed by the savages to destroy them and the Plymouth colony too. The great kindness of the Plymouth men to the chief, Massasoit, who by Winslow's medical aid and nursing was restored from what was supposed to be a fatal sickness, induced the chieftain to disclose to them the plot, on the eve of its execution.

After a careful weighing of the case, Standish was dispatched with a company of eight men to the Massachusetts tribe, where by a prompt and daring vengeance inflicted on three of the chief conspirators who had already began to whet their knives with insulting threats in his presence, he struck terror into the hearts of all. A few other Indians were slain. This was the only rupture of their peace with the savages in that generation; and for this other men were responsible. For this, the kindly Robinson wrote them a letter of warm remonstrance; but the colonists themselves were so persuaded that their existence hung upon the course they followed, that they record their special occasion for rendering "honor, praise, and glory to God for preserving us from falling when we were at the pit's brim, and feared nor knew not that we were in danger."

The poor discouraged remnants of Mr. Weston's colony took ship and sailed away, hoping to find friends and supplies at the fishing stations off the coast; while Standish furnished them "all the corn he could, scarce leaving him any to bring home; saw them well out of the bay under sail at sea, and so came home, not taking the worth of a penny of any thing that was theirs." Such was the miserable end of the party, "all able, lusty men," who came in their pride and strength, boasting of their superiority to the Plymouth company with their "many women and children and weak ones among them." "But a man's way," says Bradford, "is not in his own power: God can make the weak to stand; let him that standeth take heed lest he fall."

Not long after there came an unexpected visitor among them. He had come from England in a fishing vessel, disguised as a blacksmith, had been cast away near Portsmouth, been stripped by the Indians of every article of clothing even to his shirt, and had borrowed clothes to come to Plymouth. It was Thomas Weston, the once rich London merchant, who had come to the country only to hear of the ruin and dissolution of his colony, and to sue for kindness at the hands of this feeble band.

In their own straitened circumstances, they "remembered former courtesies," yielded to his urgent entreaties, and furnished him with beaver skins enough to set him up in trade again. They afterwards befriended him when there was a warrant out for his arrest for violating the rights of what was called the Plymouth Company in England, and the Governor even became his bail. But it is sad to relate that Mr. Weston "proved a bitter enemy to them on all occasions, and never repaid them any thing for it but reproaches and evil words." It does not appear that he ever regained his wealth, but lived as a needy adventurer, and died at Bristol, England, "in the time of the wars." His exasperation is unaccountable, except as the fruit of bitter pecuniary disappointment acting on a hot and impulsive nature, already conscious of deserved blame. But the objects of his dislike have left on record truly, that "they helped him, when all the world failed him."

A more faithful heart had ceased to beat but just before. The trusty Squanto, sole survivor of the aboriginal occupants of Plymouth, fell sick and died, "desiring the Governor to pray for him, that he might go to the Englishman's God in heaven," and bequeathing to his English friends various "remembrances of his love."

## CHAPTER XII.

### FAST AND THANKSGIVING.

The crisis was yet to come. Before the troubles about the Weymouth Colony and with the Indians were settled, the spring of 1623 had arrived. No supplies had been received. The new comers had been provided, and even the ship in which they came had been partly supplied for the home voyage. The Weymouth men had helped exhaust their provisions, and had wasted their growing crops. With the utmost difficulty the company had worried through till planting time. Small quantities of Indian corn had been procured of the natives along the coast, indeed all that could be spared; for the Indians previous to the use of English hoes, planted but little.

April came. It was evident that extraordinary measures must be taken to increase the ensuing harvest. They had learned to prize Indian corn "as more precious than silver." The experiment of laboring for the common stock, though tried by some of the best men in the world under the spur of necessity, failed to develop the best exertions. The strong man felt it an injustice to receive no more than the weaker or more indolent who did not half so much work. The more venerable members of the community felt it an indignity to be placed in their labors, food and clothing, on a level "with the meaner and younger sort." The young men repined "that they should spend their time and strength to work for other men's wives and children without any recompense;" while "for men's wives to be commanded to do service for other men, dressing their meat, washing their clothes, etc., they deemed it a kind of slavery, neither could many husbands well brook it." The whole system, forced upon them against their will, was felt to be a grievance and a source of evil, and "it would have been worse if they had been men of a different character." "Let none object," says Bradford, "that this is men's corruption, and nothing to the course itself. I answer seeing all men have this corruption in them, God in his wisdom saw another fitter course for them." He might have added that God himself implanted the desire of possession and ordained the law of property: "Thou shalt not steal—thou shalt not covet."

To meet the impending exigency and apply the utmost stimulus to exertion, it was resolved that this year every man should plant for himself. It made all hands industrious. The very women might have been seen in the field, and their children with them, planting corn. The largest possible quantity was planted. But by this time all their provisions "were spent, and they were to rest only on God's providence, at night not many times knowing where to have a bit of any thing next day. Above the people in the world," said one of them, "they had need to pray that God would give them their daily bread." And "they bore these wants," we are also told, "with great patience and alacrity of spirit."

For three months they had no bread nor any kind of grain. When the planting was passed, their solitary boat was sent out with the nets for fish, and, by relays of men, kept going all the time. Sometimes it was five or six days before she returned. When the boat was long in coming or her supply inadequate, all hands resorted to the sea-side at low-water, and dug for shell-fish in the sands; while two of the best hunters ranged the woods and brought them now and then a deer. During the winter previous they had been partly relieved by ground nuts and wild fowls.

Every hope was now centered in the young crop. The corn was well planted, according to the Indian method, with two or three fishes in every hill. It came up well. But, alas, from the third week of May for six long weeks the intense heat of summer was tempered with scarcely a drop of rain. The drought was most alarming. The earlier crop of maize began to send out the ear before the plant was half grown; and that of the later planting hung down both blade and stalk, changing its color till it seemed, and some of it proved to be dead. "Our beans also ran not up according to their wonted manner, but stood at a stay, many being parched away as though they had been scorched before the fire. Now were our hopes overthrown, and we discouraged—our joy being turned into mourning."

To add to their distress, they hear that a supply which had been sent from England had been twice driven back by the weather, and the vessel, having afterwards been seen at sea, for three months had not been heard from; only the signs of a wreck had been found on the coast. "At once God seemed to deprive us of all future hopes. The most courageous were now discouraged because God which had hitherto been our only shield and supporter, now seemed in his anger to arm himself against us."

Every good man is moved "to enter into examination of his own estate between God and his conscience;" and the whole company determine "solemnly to humble ourselves together before the Lord by fasting and prayer." To that end a day was appointed by public authority, and set apart from all other employments; hoping that the same God which had stirred us up hereunto, would be moved in mercy to look down upon us, and grant the request of our dejected souls, if our continuance there might any way stand with his glory and our good.

"But, O, the mercy of our God! who was as ready to hear as we to ask; for though in the morning when we assembled together the heavens were as clear, and the drought as like to continue, as ever it was, yet—our exercise continuing some eight or nine hours—before our departure, the weather was overcast, the clouds gathered on all sides, and on the next morning distilled such soft, sweet, and moderate showers of rain, continuing some fourteen days, that it was hard to say whether our withered corn or our drooping affections were most quickened or revived. Such was the bounty and goodness of our God." To the above narrative by Winslow, Bradford adds that the rain "came without either wind or thunder, or any violence, and by degrees in abundance, so that the earth was thoroughly wet and soaked therewith. Which did so apparently revive and quicken the decayed corn and other fruits as was wonderful to see, and made the Indians astonished to behold; and afterwards the Lord sent them such seasonable showers, with interchange of fair warm weather, as through his blessing caused a fruitful and liberal harvest to their no small comfort and rejoicing."

Three or four weeks after this time of anguish and rejoicing, two vessels arrived— the Anne and the Little James—bringing about sixty passengers. Among them were the wives and children of some who were already here, and a few others of their Leyden friends. There were also not a few who had no previous connection with them, but by side influences and importunity at London, had pressed their way in—some of them so bad, that the colony were glad to pay their expenses back again next year. The colony were still living on hope. Most of them had become quite shabby in their clothing; and "the best dish they could present their friends was a lobster or a piece of fish, without bread or any thing else but a cup of fair spring water."

The new comers were dismayed. "Some wished themselves in England again; others fell a weeping, fancying their own misery in what they saw now in others. Only some of their old friends rejoiced to see them, and that it was no worse with them—for they could not expect it should be better—and they now hoped they should enjoy better days together." All, however, with a solitary exception came in health and found the whole colony, notwithstanding their wants, in perfect health. Elder Brewster is now joined by his daughters, Fear and Patience; Samuel Fuller and several others by their wives; Robert Hickes and William Hilton by their whole families. The widow Alice Southworth came also, and in a fortnight was joined in marriage to William Bradford, who in early life, it is said, had sought her hand. Barbara Standish, the second wife of the valiant captain, came in this company; and Fear Brewster, who afterwards became the wife of Isaac Allerton.

With them came a friendly letter from Mr. Cushman; and another from a portion of the merchants—for they had some warm friends among the merchants—in which they apologize for not sending Mr. Robinson, and assure them that "the hearts of hundreds that never saw their faces are towards them" "who doubtless pray for your safety as their own."

About this time Captain Standish returns from an excursion with a supply of provisions. The vessels have come in safety with their friends. The fields are pouring out a bountiful harvest. And "having these many signs of God's favor and acceptation we thought it would be great ingratitude if secretly we should smother up the same, or content ourselves with private thanksgiving for that which by private prayer could not be obtained. And therefore another solemn day was set apart and appointed for that end, wherein we returned glory, and honor, and praise with all thankfulness to our good God which dealt so graciously with us; whose name, for these and all other mercies towards his church and chosen ones, by them be blessed and praised now and evermore. Amen."

Where and how did they keep their Thanksgiving? Some eighty rods from the water's edge in Plymouth, there rises a hill one hundred and sixty-five feet high. On the south-east portion of its summit there are still discernible marks of an old building site. From this point the eye of the Pilgrim commanded the whole region round from which the hostile Indian might approach, and gazed far off over one of the loveliest sea views in the country. Down before him he saw the placid land-locked harbor, with the island where the boat's crew, on the day before their memorable landing, kept the holy Sabbath under the shadow of a great rock; close beneath his feet the huddled cluster of rude log houses with their thatched roofs and oiled-paper windows; and between the village and the harbor, the sacred spot where in the first twelve months he laid to rest the wearied frames of half his comrades, the lovely and the strong. On this high point of view there stood, after the first eighteen months and for many years, "a large square house with a flat roof, made of thick sawn planks, stayed with oak beams"— and six four-pound cannons looking grimly round upon the top. The room below became their *meeting-house*—not their church, for the church was the company of the saints—" where they preach on Sunday and the usual holidays. They assemble" (said an eye-witness in 1627) by beat of drum, each with his musket or firelock, in front of the captain's door; they have their cloaks on, and place themselves in order three abreast, and are led by a sergeant without beat of drum. Behind comes the Governor in a long robe; on the right hand comes the preacher with his cloak on, and on the left hand the captain with his side arms and cloak, and with a small cane in his hand;— and so they march in good order, and each sets his arms down near him." After this manner, probably, they marched to their place of worship on that Thanksgiving day.

Assembled thus with the matchlock by their sides, the cannon overhead, and God all around and within, these bearded men and care-worn, great-hearted women, worshiped God in no stinted measure. "Eight or nine hours" had been the time of the Fast day's services. And though there was not such agony of wrestling to prolong the hours of Thankfulness, liberal portions of God's word no doubt were read, from the old Geneva version; words of exhortation must have flowed profusely from the heart; their prayers bore a large burden of gratitude, and doubtless they sung no asthmatic songs of praise. The *whole congregation* sang; nor for more than a hundred and fifty years did the descendants of the Pilgrims surrender the privilege of having "all the people praise God in song." They had no "lining" of the hymns. They sung no fuguing tunes. York, Windsor Martyrs, Old Hundred, and the like, they sung. Perhaps on that Thanksgiving day they sung from their own (Ainsworth's) "Book of Psalms" this very psalm:—

### Psalm C.

1. Showt to Jehovah, all the earth,
2. Serve ye Jehovah with gladness:
before him come with singing mirth
3. Know that Jehovah he God is;

> Its he that made us, and not wee ;
> his folk, and sheep of his feeding.
> 4. O with confession enter yee
> his gates, his courtyards with praising :
>
> confesse to him, blesse ye his name,
> 5. Because Jehovah he good is:
> his mercy ever is the same :
> and his faith unto all ages.

Of what took place at home that day we can only conjecture. The heartfelt acknowledgment must have gone up in many of those humble homes for perfect health, and perfect plenty, and the sight of old familiar faces, with a fervor greater than ever before. And as our fathers always carefully distinguished even in outward form a thanksgiving from a fast, so Elder Brewster must have set at home in that old arm-chair of his that is still to be seen at Pilgrim Hall, and around his festal board were ranged his children, Patience, and Fear, and Love, and

Wrestling, and Jonathan, now brought again together. The good sword of Standish with its Arabic inscription, must have been superseded by the huge kettle and the lordly dish of his that now lie peacefully by its side in Plymouth; and the pewter platters that still bear the mark, "E. W."—Edward Winslow—must have done good service. No doubt those men eat their bread with joy and drank their beverage with a merry heart; for God accepted their works. And the love of God and the spirit of overflowing gratitude crowned the feast.

Such a sad and agonizing Fast, and such a jubilant Thanksgiving day, doubtless have never come and gone since the year sixteen hundred and twenty-three.

Pilgrim Church.   pp. 240.

## CHAPTER XIII.

### REST AT LAST.

THE crisis was past. Never again was the Plymouth colony reduced to such straits, nor its existence seriously jeoparded. The colonists labored under many disadvantages, but the Lord blessed them and they prospered. When the seven years were ended, they bought out the London merchants for 1,800 pounds. Every foot of their lands, to the time of king Philip's war, was procured of the Indians by purchase. They expended many hundred pounds in bringing over the remainder of the Leyden company and providing for them in New England. And at length, in the year 1630, the last of that band were brought in safety to their brethren in Plymouth.

But before their emigration was completed, other men had followed on their track. In 1629 and 1630 commenced those settlements at Salem, Boston, and the neighboring regions, that filled the State of Massachusetts with a wealthy and powerful body of colonists. The Plymouth settlers were few in number, and feeble in resources; strong only in their brave hearts, their admirable spirit, their indomitable energy, and their firm faith in God. But it was their honorable privilege to have opened the way, and drawn all eyes after them. As early as 1623, a portion of the merchants who sympathized with them, wrote to them thus: " Let it not be grievous unto you that you have been instruments to break the ice for others who come after with less difficulty. The honor shall be yours to the world's end. We bear you always in our breasts, and our hearty affection is towards you all, *as are the hearts of hundreds who never saw your faces*, who doubtless pray for your safety as their own, as we ourselves both do and ever shall, that the same God which hath so marvelously preserved you from seas, foes, and famine, will still preserve you from all future dangers, and make you honorable among men and glorious in bliss at the last day." The settlers of Salem distinctly state that the tidings from the Plymouth men "occasioned other men to take knowledge of the place and to take it into consideration."

When, therefore, the oppressions that king James laid upon the Puritans began to be aggravated by his misguided son, Charles I., and the fierce archbishop Laud, New England was the place of rest to which at once they turned their eyes. The Salem church was immediately drawn into friendly relations to the Plymouth church; and when Skelton and Higginson were ordained as pastor and teacher at Salem, Governor Bradford gave the right hand of fellowship.

In their own church affairs the Plymouth church met with much opposition from a portion of the London merchants. Mr. Robinson had expected soon to follow his flock to America. Indeed he seems to have remained behind with much reluctance. Elder Brewster meanwhile was the preacher to the Plymouth church; but from some scruples of his own and Mr. Robinson's, he never administered baptism nor the Lord's Supper. But Robinson's coming, which was dependant on the merchants who furnished funds, was continually delayed. At length it appeared that a strong and influential faction of the merchants was resolutely bent on giving an Episcopalian ministry to the little church, or, at least, determined that such a man as the Leyden pastor should not join his flock.

It will be remembered how on the departure of the Mayflower company, Mr. Robinson had spoken of his earnest desire "to have borne his part with them in their first brunt," and of himself as held back by "strong necessity," but having his "better part with them." The next year he writes to them, "My most earnest desire is unto you; from whom I will not longer keep, (if God will,) than means can be procured to bring me with the wives and children of divers of you, and the rest of your brethren, whom I could not leave behind me without great injury both to you and to them, and offence to God and all men. The death of so many of our dear friends and brethren, oh! how grievous hath it been to you to bear, and to us to take knowledge of." Eighteen months later the merchants apologize for the delay in sending "him on whom you most depend;" and in the beginning of 1624 they plainly inform the colonists that there is a strong faction among them firmly opposed to the coming of Mr. Robinson. That faction send over a preacher, one John

Lyford, who at first ingratiates himself with the church, but is soon found to be in correspondence with the enemies of Robinson in England, to prevent his coming, as well as writing bitter slanders of the colony. Further investigation proves him to be a man of immoral life, and he is rejected from the colony.

About this time Mr. Robinson begins to be fully informed of the state of affairs, and in December, 1623, he writes to Bradford that "our hopes of coming unto you are small, and weaker than ever." He has discovered, as he writes to Brewster at the same date, that "five or six of the adventurers are absolutely bent for us, above any others," that the great body of them are "honestly-minded and lovingly disposed towards us," but so connected with certain "forward preachers" as to be virtually controlled by them; and that "five or six of them are our bitter professed adversaries," and unwilling "that I of all others should be transported. And for these adversaries, if they have but half the wit to their malice, they will stop my course when they see it intended, for which this delaying serveth them very opportunely. And as one restive jade can hinder by hanging back, more than two or three can draw forward, so will it be in this case." The whole letter seems almost entirely hopeless in regard to his coming, and closes, "Your God and ours, and the God of all his, bring us together if it be his will, and keep us in the meanwhile and always to his glory, and make us serviceable to his majesty and faithful to the end. Amen."

Robinson's prediction probably would have been happily disappointed and he would have been relieved from his "languishing state," as he terms it, but the time was then rapidly approaching for his journey to a better country, even an heavenly. All that is known of his peaceful end is contained in a letter from one of his bereaved flock at Leyden.

"Loving and kind friends," writes Roger White to Governor Bradford and Elder Brewster, April 28, 1625, "I know not whether this will ever come to your hand, or miscarry as other my letters have done; yet in regard of the Lord's dealings here, I have had a great desire to write unto you, knowing your desire to bear a part with us, both in our joys and sorrows, as we do with you. These are therefore to give you to understand that it hath pleased the Lord to take out of this vale of tears, your and our loving and faithful pastor, and my dear and Reverend brother, Mr. John Robinson, who was sick some eight days. He began to be sick on Saturday, in the morning, yet the next day (being Lord's day) he taught us twice. And so the week after he grew weaker, every day more than other; yet he felt no pain but weakness all the time of his sickness. The physic he took wrought kindly in man's judgment; but he grew weaker every day, feeling little or no pain, and sensible to the very last. He fell sick the 22d of February, and departed this life the 1st of March. He had a continual inward ague, yet free from infection, so that all his friends came freely to him. And if either prayers, tears or means could have saved his life, he had not gone hence. But he having faithfully finished his course, and performed his work which the Lord had appointed him here to do, now resteth with the Lord in eternal happiness. We wanting him and all church government, yet still by the mercy of God continue and hold close together, in peace and quietness; and so hope we shall do, though we be very weak. Wishing (if such were the will of God) that you and we were again united together in one either there or here; but seeing it is the will of the Lord thus to dispose of things, we must labor with patience to rest contented till it pleases the Lord otherwise to dispose."

"The Lord took him away," wrote Thomas Blossom, another of his church, "even as fruit falleth before it is ripe; when neither length of days nor infirmity of body did seem to call for his end. . . . Alas, you would fain have had him with you, and he would as fain have come to you. Many letters and much speech hath been about his coming to you, but never any solid course propounded for his going; if the course propounded the last year had appeared to have been certain, he would have gone though with two or three families. I know no man among us knew his mind better than I did about those things; he was loth to leave the church, yet I know also that he would have accepted the worst conditions which in the largest extent of a good conscience could be taken, to have come to you." But the Lord had a better thing in store for him.

Twenty-seven days later died of the tertian ague, James of England, who had "harried" Robinson out of the land; and about the same time Robert Cushman died in England, who, after the first panic at Southampton, had been the firm and useful friend of the colony.

It pleased God to spare William Brewster in good health to a very great age. He shared all the toils and sufferings of his brethren, in their days of darkness, with a cheerful spirit. And afterwards so long as he was able, he continued to "labor with his hands in the fields," and "when the church had no other minister, he taught twice on every Sabbath and that both powerfully and profitably." He lived to see other churches formed all around, in Duxbury, Scituate, Sandwich, Yarmouth, Barnstable, Marshfield and Taunton, and to witness the occupation of all the chief points in Massachusetts and Connecticut by a powerful body of settlers, who came direct from England, blessed with a learned and able ministry. Mather, and Cotton, and Hooker, and Davenport, and Eliot, and their noble brethren were here. More than fifty towns and villages were settled; and the confederacy was forming between the four colonies of Plymouth, Massachusetts, New Haven and Connecticut. Brewster's son Jonathan, destined for the ministry, had graduated at Harvard University in 1642; and in the year after this great joy, the old man passed away to his rest.

"I am about to begin this year," writes Governor Bradford in 1643, "with that which was a matter of great sadness and mourning unto them all. About the 18th of April died their Reverend Elder, and my dear and loving friend, Mr. William Brewster; a man that had done and suffered much for the Lord Jesus and the gospel's sake, and had borne his part in weal and woe with this poor, persecuted church, above thirty-six years in England, Holland, and in this wilderness, and done the Lord and them faithful service in his place and calling. And notwithstanding the many troubles and sorrows he passed through, the Lord upheld him to a great age. He was near fourscore years of age (if not all out) when he died. He had this blessing added by the Lord to all the rest, to die in his bed, in peace, in the midst of his friends, who mourned and wept over him, and ministered what help and comfort they could unto him, and he again re-comforted them whilst he could. His sickness was not long, and to the last day thereof he did not wholly keep his bed. His speech continued till somewhat more than half a day, and then failed him; and about nine or ten o'clock that evening he died, without any pangs at all. A few hours before, he drew his breath short, and some minutes before his last, he drew his breath long, as a man fallen into a sound sleep without any pangs or gaspings, and so sweetly departed this life unto a better."

A large number of those who passed through the hardships of the first winter and spring lived to a good old age. God permitted them to witness the fruits of their self-denials and sufferings before he called them away. Thirty of them were spared for thirty years. Twelve of them were living sixty years after the landing; and one of them, Mary Allerton, the widow of Robert Cushman's son Thomas, was living seventy-eight years from that memorable time.

Standish, Winslow, Allerton and Bradford lived till Cromwell was fairly seated on the throne of the Tudors and the Stuarts, and perfect religious toleration was established for a time in England. Then at a good old age they dropped away within four or five years of each other. In 1655 Edward Winslow died at sea, at the age of sixty years. He had been a most honored and useful member of the new Commonwealth, and a trusted agent in its affairs abroad. His estate in Marshfield became, in later years, the favorite country seat of Daniel Webster. The next year Standish "fell asleep in the Lord," at his home in Duxbury —a place that was named by him for his old ancestral home in England. He was more than seventy years of age.

The ensuing year Bradford followed his ancient comrades. For thirty-one years he had been the honored Governor of the colony,—having been excused for five years only after the death of Carver, and that upon his own urgent request. For several months his health was infirm and failing, till in May, 1657, he was seized with acute disease. The last night but one of his life, his mind was so enraptured by contemplations upon religious truth and the hopes of futurity, that he said to his friends in the morning, "The good Spirit of God has given me a pledge of my happiness in another world, and the first fruits of eternal glory." And he passed to his rest, greatly lamented throughout New England.

Thirteen years longer lingered his widow, Alice Southworth Bradford. She had fled with her father to Holland, probably at the age of seventeen; had shared all the joys and sorrows of the colony at Plymouth except those of the first eighteen months; and now passed to her rest at the ripe age of eighty years. Her life had been one of exemplary activity and great usefulness; and her memory left a long traditional fragrance in the colony. Inside the cover of the recently discovered manuscript of her husband's history, some affectionate hand, long since mouldered to dust, pasted a copy of rude verses on " the life and death of that godly matron, Mistress Alice Bradford," narrating her history, commemorating

"Her holy, blessed, heavenly example,"

and lamenting the gradual dropping away of those elder saints :—

"'Tis sad to see our houses dispossessed
Of holy saints, whose memory is blest;
When they decease, and closéd are in tomb,
There's few or none that rises in their room,
That's like to them in holiness and grace—
Which makes our times look with so sad a face.
Her glass is run, her work is done, and she
Is happy unto all eternity."

Thus one by one they disappeared from the earth. The last of the Mayflower passengers lived till there were a hundred and thirty churches, and more than a hundred thousand inhabitants in New England; till two editions of Eliot's Indian Bible had been printed, and thirty Indian churches had been formed in Massachusetts, with about "three thousand praying Indians."

In looking back on the history of that memorable band, the chief thing that impresses us is their FIRM, CHEERFUL FAITH IN GOD. That was their light, and their strength. They had little else. They were few; they were poor; they had little influence; they were without friends; they had no men of renown to lead them on. Never, since the days of the apostles, perhaps, did a feebler band lead off a greater enterprise. Never did an enterprise seem to human eyes more absolutely hedged with difficulties at every step. It is worth studying for the very purpose of seeing over what obstacles and through whatever impending defeat all those momentous movements were carried on. At each step the way seemed shut before them; and the only light they had came from their calm assurance that God would take care of them so long as they walked the plain path of duty. Never were men more confiding in God, and never did men more fully own his hand in every daily mercy. They "sought direction" from him before every decision. They returned thanks to him for every mercy. They believed in a *daily providence* that gave them daily bread, and saved their lives from the Indian arrows, and poured out the rain on their withering crops, and numbered the very hairs of their head. And they felt safe because they knew God was with them. "They rested on his Providence," say they, "and knew whom they believed."

Look at their continual frustrations and discouragements. Twice baffled in the attempt to leave England, with much loss of property and distress. Forced again to sacrifice their worldly prospects for spiritual peace, by quitting Amsterdam. Oppressed with penury at Leyden, and worn out with perpetual solicitudes. Met with dismal apprehensions on the first proposal to seek another home. Too poor to plant the colony they decide upon, and obliged to submit to the most forbidding terms. Frustrated in their efforts to obtain a pledge of toleration, and again obliged "herein to rest upon God's providence." Delayed by bickerings in the Plymouth company till the zeal of the merchants was cooled off. Left in such uncertainty that six weeks before they sailed, neither money nor vessels were provided for their transportation. Ill-equipped, at last. Incurring the anger of the chief merchant adventurer on the eve of their sailing. Wasting precious time and scanty provisions, in vexatious delays on the English coast, and obliged at last to part with the vessel they had bought for the use of their new home. Setting sail amid predictions of utter defeat from their chief agent in England, himself declining to share their fate. Failing to reach their destination, and landed in midwinter on a bleak shore, with disaffection muttering among them, and a selfish crew anxious to get rid of them. Then came the forlorn task of founding a settlement amid the frosts of winter, and under continual apprehension of the savages. Then followed the heart-sickening calamity that laid low one-half their number. New settlers came to increase their numbers, but to diminish their supplies. Tidings occasionally came across the waters, of trouble and opposition in the London company. A reckless band exhausted their provisions and endangered their existence. Then came the famine.

But amid all these things their faith never failed. When extinction seemed to come and look in their faces, they never lost confidence in God. They felt that *they had forsaken God;* and again they drew near to him with agonizing prayer. And then their sorrow was turned into great and exceeding joy. The Lord heard them—and they said, let his holy "name be blessed and praised now and forevermore." It was a simple, confiding, daily faith, that saw God in every thing, that laid hold of his hand, and "walked with God." It was well expressed at Leyden when in reply to all the difficulties foreseen and admitted, they simply said, "Our ends are good and honorable, our calling lawful and urgent, and therefore we may expect the blessing of God in our proceeding. Yea, though we should lose our lives in this action, yet we may have comfort in so doing; and our *endeavors* will be honorable."

Nothing but such a faith was adequate to such an enterprise. Any other spirit would have completely failed. When the Mayflower returned to England after the first winter's terrible mortality, no one proposed to return in her. Just one hundred and one years before saw the fleet of Cortez, by order of the commander, burned and sunk in the harbor of Vera Cruz, to shut himself and his army in Mexico. It has been recorded as one of the most daring deeds in the history of the world. Yet though they were nigh seven hundred strong, able-bodied men, all armed to the teeth, it required all the address of their general to save him from the despairing vengeance of his soldiers. But here was a little band of fifty, including women and children, still weak from sickness, living in their mud-plastered log-huts, with their dead sleeping behind them all hidden in the bank, and the wilderness and the savages before them, quietly watching the breaking of the last bond that bound them to their native land. There must have been tearful eyes that followed those white sails disappearing in the distant blue. But there were stout hearts beneath, that turned resolutely and cheerfully to their lot.

The lesson is worth pondering both by the young and by the old, to see through what continual and seemingly insuperable obstacles, great and good things are accomplished, and how they that will do good in this world must often walk by faith, and not by sight. And the inner history of a great multitude of achievements for the cause of Christ would teach the same lesson.

For, how wonderfully God was working with these humble men, and even by these adverse events, to accomplish a noble work. These men thought only of doing their duty in a very humble way. They had no grand schemes in mind. They never even dreamed, to the day of their death, what a work they had begun. They felt that they owed something to their children, to themselves, and to their Master in heaven; and they went quietly and trustfully about their Father's business. They did not at the time understand the way in which God was leading them. The persecution that drove them from England, no doubt they felt to be an unmitigated hardship. The time spent in Holland may have seemed to them lost time. The difficulties that delayed their expedition, and the poverty that cramped it, were a sore trial to them. The delays in England, the loss of the Speedwell, the trouble with the merchants, they would gladly have been spared. The sickness and famine were a dark visitation. But God's hand was in all these things. They would not have left England except as they were driven out. The residence in Holland was a necessary preparation for their further work; it enlarged their views, bound them together, inured them to hardships and made them willing to undertake the distant expedition. All the delays and difficulties that made the enterprise most forbidding, sifted their number, and left the choice seed alone. The sorrows and trials of the first settlement not only kept them near to God, but shut them up from all intrusion, and left them to work out their experiment unmolested. And at every step of their winding way, when the path before appeared at its end, God always unfolded it as they went on. Hill after hill seemed to shut down across their track; but whenever they reached the spot, the way went winding on among the hills. Sometimes it was only at the last moment that the obstruction was removed. Sometimes it was done in the common course of events; at others, by such unexpected methods as powerfully to enforce their views of a special providence.

And thus step by step, through perplexities and trials, and difficulties and opposition, God led them on and they humbly followed, till their noble work was done. So shall it be with every high achievement. It is not done in dream-land, amid flowers and sunshine and luxury and applause; but in the hard prose scenes of daily life, with struggling and weariness, and self-denial, and many a discouragement. But toil and faith and patience, with the blessing of God, will make their mark.

"Trust in the Lord and do good; so shalt thou dwell in the land, and verily thou shalt be fed. Delight thyself also in the Lord; and he shall give thee the desires of thine heart. Commit thy way unto the Lord; trust also in him, and he shall bring it to pass."

THE END.

www.ingramcontent.com/pod-product-compliance
Lightning Source LLC
Chambersburg PA
CBHW031946230426
43672CB00010B/2072